Speaking One's Soul

*Magnifying God's Word
in a Madly Godless World*

Patti Hershwitzky
Mary Sobel Ott

⊕ENROUTE
Make the time

En Route Books and Media, LLC
5705 Rhodes Avenue
St. Louis, MO 63109

Contact us at **contactus@enroutebooksandmedia.com**

Cover Credit: Mary Ott
Copyright 2025 Patti Hershwitzky and Mary Ott

ISBN-13: 979-8-88870-363-2
Library of Congress Control Number: 2025930731

All rights reserved. No part of this book may be reproduced, stored in a retrieval system, or transmitted in any form, or by any means, electronic, mechanical, photocopying, or otherwise, without the prior written permission of the author.

Table of Contents

Introduction & Framework 1

Foreword on the Cardinal Virtues 13

Section 1: The Joyful Mysteries - Emphasis on Temperance 14

	Joyful Mystery- Traditional Virtue (Fruit)	Associated Contemporary Reflection	15
a.	The Annunciation - Humility	Prayerful Silence vs. Social Media	15
b.	The Visitation - Love of Neighbor	Subsidiarity-Solidarity vs. Collectivism	27
c.	The Nativity - Poverty of Spirit	Spirit of Poverty vs. Possessiveness	37
d.	The Presentation - Obedience	Universal Obedience vs. World Compliance	45
e.	Finding of Jesus in Temple - Piety	Jesus's Teaching vs. Public Education	55

Section 2: The Luminous Mysteries -Emphasis on Prudence 64

	Luminous Mystery-Traditional Virtue (Fruit)	Associated Contemporary Reflection	65
a.	The Baptism of Jesus - Openness to the Holy Spirit	Fidelity to Faith vs. Loyalty to State	65
b.	The Wedding at Cana - To Jesus through Mary	Holy Motherhood vs. Fatherless Homes	75
c.	Establishment of the Kingdom of God - Trust in God	Just Immigration vs. Chaotic Intrusion	85
d.	The Transfiguration - Holiness	Transformation vs. Transgendered	97
e.	Institution of the Eucharist - Eucharistic Adoration	Union with God vs. World Uniformity	109

Table of Contents v

Section 3: The Sorrowful Mysteries - Emphasis on Fortitude.. 120

	Sorrowful Mystery- Traditional Virtue (Fruit)	Associated Contemporary Reflection	121
a.	The Agony in the Garden - Contrition	Contrition (Self) vs. Condemnation (Others)	121
b.	The Scourging - Making Compromises and Accepting Suffering	Fruits of Chastity vs. Rot of Lust	133
c.	The Crowning of Thorns - Moral Courage	Meekness vs. Cowardliness	145
d.	The Carrying of the Cross - Patience	Perseverance vs. Resentment	155
e.	The Crucifixion - Salvation	Surrender to God vs. Resignation to Evil	165

Section 4: The Glorious Mysteries - Emphasis on Justice... 178

	Glorious Mystery- Traditional Virtue (Fruit)	Associated Contemporary Reflection	179
a.	The Resurrection - Faith	Faith in Salvation Education vs. Public Education	179
b.	The Ascension - Hope	Rightful Hope vs. Temporal Hope	189
c.	The Descent of the Holy Spirit - Wisdom	Wisdom of the Word vs. Worldly Cleverness	199
d.	The Assumption - Marian Devotion	Peaceful Life & Death vs. Euthanasia	209
e.	The Crowning of Mary as Queen - Eternal Happiness	Just Rule vs. Earthly Monarchs	221

Resources by Section and Chapter 233

Patricia (Patti) Hershwitzky's Author Bio 261

Mary Ott's Author Bio 261

I came to bring fire to the earth,
and how I wish it were already kindled!
(Luke 12:49)

Introduction and Framework

Blending Traditional Virtues with Contemporary Reflections for Individual Rosary Devotion

Contemporary (modern) and traditional are two contrasting styles which can be observed in various aspects of life, including art, architecture, lifestyle choices, and religion. Traditional religious practices are often rooted in cultural and religious beliefs which emphasize family, faith, and humility. Traditional Catholic practices place a strong emphasis on rituals and concepts that have been understood and practiced for centuries. In contrast, living one's Catholic faith in a contemporary world has its inherent challenges and pitfalls.

By uniting the traditional practice of saying the rosary with its mystery and virtue (fruit) joined with a modern moral snare or vice, which can vex even the average Catholic, any individual can enrich their rosary practice by making the devotion more customized. We seek to help other Catholics, and new or returning faith seekers, to overcome their current daily challenges by finding prayerful solutions to their personal snares, daily temptations, or situational stumbles which keep them from deepening their faith in God.

Understanding how to overcome modern day issues using this rosary devotion, Catholics might be able to discern much deeper meaning from the fruits of the mysteries of the rosary. Our unique life experiences and our own individual expression of love for our faith and praying the rosary can help us to spiritually battle against contemporary desires, harmful habits, and societal snares. Each one of us can live a faith-based spiritual life by seeking the salvation God so mercifully wants to give to us.

In this modern world, people are exhausted by economic pressures. Many are excessively emotional over vitriolic politics and polarizing politicians or furious with unresolved social issues. Others are seething with irritation towards secular neighbors. Or weeping at the thought of wayward loved ones who are in danger of losing their pathway to God. In short, people are more reactive and alternating between peaceful kindness to frustration when faced with agnostic propaganda. And let us not neglect to mention the incessant streaming of internet click-bait temptations that arise from artificial intelligence (AI). AI is intended to disrupt our daily lives and charitable senses at every turn by forcing upon us social media sycophants who crave constant attention, by any means, to satiate ego-driven needs.

But you are CATHOLIC! A person, presumably, who is serenely faithful, joyfully hopeful, and globally charitable… even toward your enemies. You are prayerful and trying so very hard to keep yourself in God's presence and attain heaven, not just in some distant future, but on a daily basis. Ardently you seek to communicate truth to those around you, *knowing* that the world deceives, life is short, and eternity is…well…forever. Yet, the overwhelming majority of the world not only turns a deaf ear, but attacks with foul language and spiteful ridicule. It feels as if so many in the world are bent on crushing the dedicated faithful and the Church underfoot. Ask yourself as we did as sisters, isn't it easier to stay silent? To remain securely tucked into the safe shadows of our faith, behind closed doors, than it is to emerge into the vulnerable space of public opinion and speak out with fearlessness like Christ did? If you understand these feelings, you are not alone!

We are sisters, Patti Hershwitzky and Mary (Sobel) Ott, but also wives, mothers, and grandmothers, at the opposite ends of the Baby Boomer spectrum, who rediscovered our Faith and our sisterhood in Jesus Christ, and noted similar observations about a world gone mad.

The world appears to be undergoing a designed chaos intended to upend peaceful community life and the constructive exchange of ideas and discourse. Also due to many communications with others, we have experienced universal frustration trying to live our faith in a world that despises courageous Christianity *even though Jesus Christ gave us fair warning.*

Initially, Patti decided to speak up *as a Catholic* in a book on current politics. This was based somewhat on her own political science background, experience with campaigns, and engagement with various community organizations. Patti first began with all good intentions of reaching Catholics and other Christians with a guide to making healthy political choices but was incredibly frustrated with both major political parties and the often misguided and shortsighted perceptions on major issues. Initially, possible book titles of, "If I were U.S. Senator…" or "Speaking My Mind" were considered.

After many attempts to grapple with and respond to the increasingly strident and often combative nature of contemporary politics and the incredible polarization and apostasy even within parishes, Patti concluded that the scales had tipped too far. Then, she focused more deliberately on the matter spiritually. *How can our soul express itself in faithful unity with the Holy Spirit and The Word?* Patti also concluded through prayer and productive silence that, while the

Sacrifice of the Holy Mass is still the singular most redemptive work, the power of the Scriptural Rosary remains one of the greatest modes of reflecting on critical issues, forming good conscience and solid opinion, and then acting upon inspirations grounded in that most effective prayer, particularly for individual souls. Thus evolved: **Speaking One's Soul**.

As always, God has a bigger plan. And that was to include Patti's sister, Mary, in this book project.

***

Mary's story is as follows…

As a younger sister, I have always looked to Patti's courage and dedication to her faith, though not knowing her personal struggles. She appeared an example of what our parents taught us growing up: Faith first, then everything else. However, the reality of life and the different twists and turns of our lives separated us. Not just spiritually, but geographically. I am nine years younger than Patti. My faith journey was placed on hold by my own doing. Life as a mother, wife, working person, and paying the bills became my priority. Honest disclosure: I let my relationship with God go cold. The education I received in Catholic school did not seem to aid in understanding how to apply the basic knowledge of my faith in a concrete manner so that I could continue to grow my soul while navigating very modern, complicated life challenges. The only time I did not go to Catholic school was high school. I graduated from a Catholic college. Yet, I fell victim to the influences of a more geographically progressive community and lifestyle. What was my yardstick to determine if I was a 'good' Catholic: How many of the ten commandments have I broken? *The understanding of my Catholic faith was truly a fragile weave made from thin fibers.*

Candidly, as each commandment was broken…over the years, I fell further away from my cradle faith. I became dismissive of religious dogma and defeated by my human weakness. Then, I got angry at the church following sexual scandals within the priesthood of the church. These scandals justified my falling away even more. Or so I thought. As God would have it…in the quiet moments of my dealing with divorce, grief, breast cancer, chemotherapy, and a few other life altering experiences, I started to come back to Him—*privately*—in a closed room away from family. Yes—I am His prodigal child. Humility offers a cathartic transformation of the soul; accepting one's brokenness ignites one's resolve to seek reconciliation. My brokenness gave birth to an examination of conscience. Grace is the gift of accepting His forgiveness and mercy. I truly fell in love with Jesus. He is my Lord and Savior. Miracles never cease as I continue to experience His tangible presence in my life every day. The Lord is a tender Savior whose heart and wounds burn with flames of hope for us while He waits patiently for our return.

Now, in my sixties, I see a modern world more hammered by ominous influences gripping the hearts of our youth while peddling a pseudo-intellectual, quasi-religious, global-political mandate to the masses through social media. I feel society is exponentially more easily manipulated since the introduction of 24/7 'media' access. It began with my children and their interaction with the internet in the 1990s. I witnessed what started out as a wonderful tool for information and educational research become a festering haven for monetizing and creating immoral or fraudulent platforms. I put parental controls in place on the computer. But….then came the *real evil* which is boldly living on the internet and chasing down innocent souls via the mobile phone environment. It's like a global feeding frenzy now.

And because of this and so much more, the time to reach out to souls for salvation is now! The sower and the reaper will rejoice together.

***

So, **Speaking One's Soul** is more about what we should have learned through a life solidly immersed in truth. The ugly stains of current politics can only be revealed in the light of faith. Society's demise can only be salvaged by acknowledging that life today is more cadaverous than alive, and only Divine Mercy (grace) can heal the deadly wounds threatening to pull us into an inescapable abyss. The most powerful tool, the rosary, can be our salvation and "circle of life".

In order to live peacefully in faith, we still must "walk the walk," starting with a breakfast of spiritual champions. Attending daily Mass is a viable option for many, but not for all. *We should include the Old and New Testament as it interconnects, foretells, and unfolds the history of man with God.* Our great saints provide uplifting wisdom and guidance. Just reading the Church's love letters can set our minds and souls at rest. We have as our peaceful shepherd the Son of God. The Holy Souls in Purgatory assist…

So that we remain steadfastly in hope, we must focus on the object of our hope continuously throughout the day and concentrate on the lives of those who overcame severe temptations and trials and converted their lives to reach everlasting joy. For the more busy among us, note that even brief prayers throughout the day empower our spirit. And, finally, by keeping our gaze on the Holy Face of Jesus, we may genuinely love and pray for our neighbors, even those who give us the most sorrow or even hold us in contempt.

A SPECIAL NOTE: To our non-Catholic brothers and sisters whom we so lovingly entreat to pray this "circle of life," kindly be assured that The Rosary glorifies God by meditating on the Mysteries of our Our Savior's life, passion, death, and resurrection. It is a Scriptural prayer foremost, including the initial Our Father and Glory Be. Yet, that is also true for the Hail Mary, which communicates our reverence for the Mother of God (and our mother), and a plea for our maternal protector to plea for the Mercy of her Son!

The Framework for "Speaking One's Soul"

In this book, the common order within each section and chapter of a Mystery includes: the respective contemporary snare and vice; contemplative reflection; a model saint to imitate; the author's personal narratives relating to stumbling in their faith; a contemporary role model; a conversion story; rosary and prayer intentions of your own to reflect upon. Resources used for or complementary to each section and chapter are found at the back of the book. There are four sections in this book and five chapters within each section.

Each chapter focuses on the Life of Jesus Christ according to the Mysteries of the Holy Rosary, from the Joyful to the Luminous, to the Sorrowful, and concluding with the Glorious Mysteries. Each Mystery focuses on spiritually navigating a contemporary point of tension.

Overall, each of these four themes (sections) expound on a particular cardinal virtue:

JOYFUL: Temperance because in all matters Mary and Joseph modeled temperance, highlighting subordinate virtues of humility, charity, detachment from materialism, obedience, and pursuit of the Good, True, and Beautiful;

LUMINOUS: Prudence because in the Light is perfect wisdom—though sometimes hidden from human reason—to bring each of us to transformation in Jesus Christ;

SORROWFUL: Emphasizing fortitude, extraordinary strength through trial, as our current culture necessitates courage. Most of us will not suffer a red martyrdom, but most of us will at least foresee the tsunami of white martyrdom. Today, thousands if not millions of souls, particularly outside our country endure the most intense cruelties, matching if not exceeding anything in past history;

GLORIOUS: Justice which seeks the good of the other—what is due them— is not human justice although different times in history judges have shown greater allegiance to God and His Word. It is particularly painful that what passes for justice today is actually partisan politics, often prosecutorial and punitive towards perceived enemies of the State.

Furthermore, each Mystery extols the King and Queen of Heaven. Other descendent virtues correspond, and an intentional effort was made to incorporate those. Accompanying each Mystery with its virtue (fruit) is an associated contemporary reflection according to each focus in the Life of Jesus Christ. True life narratives express the snares of sin but also salvation by virtue. This book presents traditional virtues with contemporary snares (temptations) for individual rosary devotion.

Next, the advice of holy persons can lead readers to contemplate how to act in the world and aspire to heaven. Concluding each chapter is a conversion story highlighting a person who either converted or returned to the one true faith, often from the near abyss. Resources at the back of the book include helpful associations, apostolates, and organizations to provide support in times of despair or doubt. There is a plethora of such and growing daily!

What is the Personal Rosary?

The concept of the *person*alized Rosary, particularly weaved for this age, speaks to the crisis in our individual natures as we each are made in the image and likeness of God. Our souls, like our fingerprints, are unduplicated in any other being. Moreover, though Holy Baptism removes the stain of Original Sin, each of us still suffers from an inclination to sin, called concupiscence. One source of temptation is found in the created world. Political and social structures can place us in many precarious spiritual battlefields—judging people by their affiliations where we can easily lose sight of their unique personhood. (CCC 405-409)

The personal Rosary is most versatile when focusing on one's self and other individuals, too. One may pray for one person throughout or several persons. Each of the ten beads is representative of self, first, not in a falsely self-serving manner but needing to start in a place of humility. In next order are spouses or close friends; family; neighbors; clergy and religious; educators; health care workers; business persons (including attorneys); politicians (elected and appointed); and public figures including communicators and entertainers.

There will be ample opportunities to pray this personalized Rosary in myriad ways. There will be days when one issue may preoccupy your mind, but consider persons in need of a particular virtue surrounding that concern. The entire premise of the *person*alized Rosary is to intercede for persons, *not* always issues, per se, and particularly those most in danger of death without repentance. Be flexible and not fixated. This is not formalistic or prescriptive but a healing balm. **Following the prudence of St. Francis de Sales, these pray times need not be laborious or obsessively followed.**

Our lives are often exceedingly busy, if not overwhelming at times. However, by disciplining oneself to start with prayer and devotion, later prayers follow almost naturally. Even on choppy prayer days, you will "pick up" special intentions. When the Rosary is not well said or completed, offer it up. Saints have attested to God's close proximity even while being themselves distracted. **Do NOT be anxious about these occasions.** The more you prioritize, the easier it becomes, and the more you will discover that you love your prayer time. Also, do not be surprised to find news, and other depressing channels of communication, including social media, the thorns in your side that can only be removed by quietly removing yourself to a mini retreat in the bedroom or taking a walk.

As to the "repetitiveness" of the Hail Mary, realize that this provides a continuous stream of petitions, not unlike the refrain of our most popular hymns, and overlaying a rhythmic tenor to the Rosary. However, prayer on each bead with a special intention, while meditating on Scripture, is most pleasing to God. **Speaking One's Soul** will then evolve naturally—you will see that. You will also become a better self-detector when your anxiety, anger, and exasperation are rearing their ugly heads. No, that will not go away completely, anymore than temptation and tribulations will disappear.

God promises peace to His children of good will, but that does not dispel adversity to help us grow closer to Him and bring others close to Him. As noted in Daily Catholic Wisdom (2/17/2024) in the words of St. Augustine of Hippo: *We have to reprimand the undisciplined, console the fainthearted, support the weak, refute the opponents, be wary of the clever, instruct the ignorant, stir up the lazy, thwart the belligerent, retrain the proud, appease the quarreling, help the needy, liberate the oppressed, encourage the good, tolerate the wicked, and love everyone.*

Remember, we are good soldiers of Christ.

'My son,' says the Savior Christ, 'I must be the end of all your works if you desire to be happy and blessed. If you refer all goodness to me, from Whom all goodness comes, then all your inward affections will be purified and made clean, which otherwise would be evil and centered on yourself and other creatures.'

(Imitation of Christ, *How All Things are to be Referred to God, as to the End of Every Work*)

Foreword on the Cardinal Virtues

Aside from an abundance of resources on the topic, the Catechism of the Catholic Church (CCC) provides a wealth of knowledge about the theological (Faith, Hope, Charity), cardinal, and moral virtues. The Church has identified the four cardinal virtues: Prudence, Justice, Fortitude, and Temperance. These four virtues are known as "hinge virtues" because all the subcategorized virtues link to them. The twenty virtues most often related to the Holy Rosary's four Mystery sets (Joyful, Luminous, Sorrowful, and Glorious) likewise descend in multiple, interconnected ways from these. However, only one cardinal virtue will be expanded upon in each set. The reader is encouraged to study how each of the other cardinal virtues may apply to a particular Mystery and to the contemporary subject of reflection in each chapter.

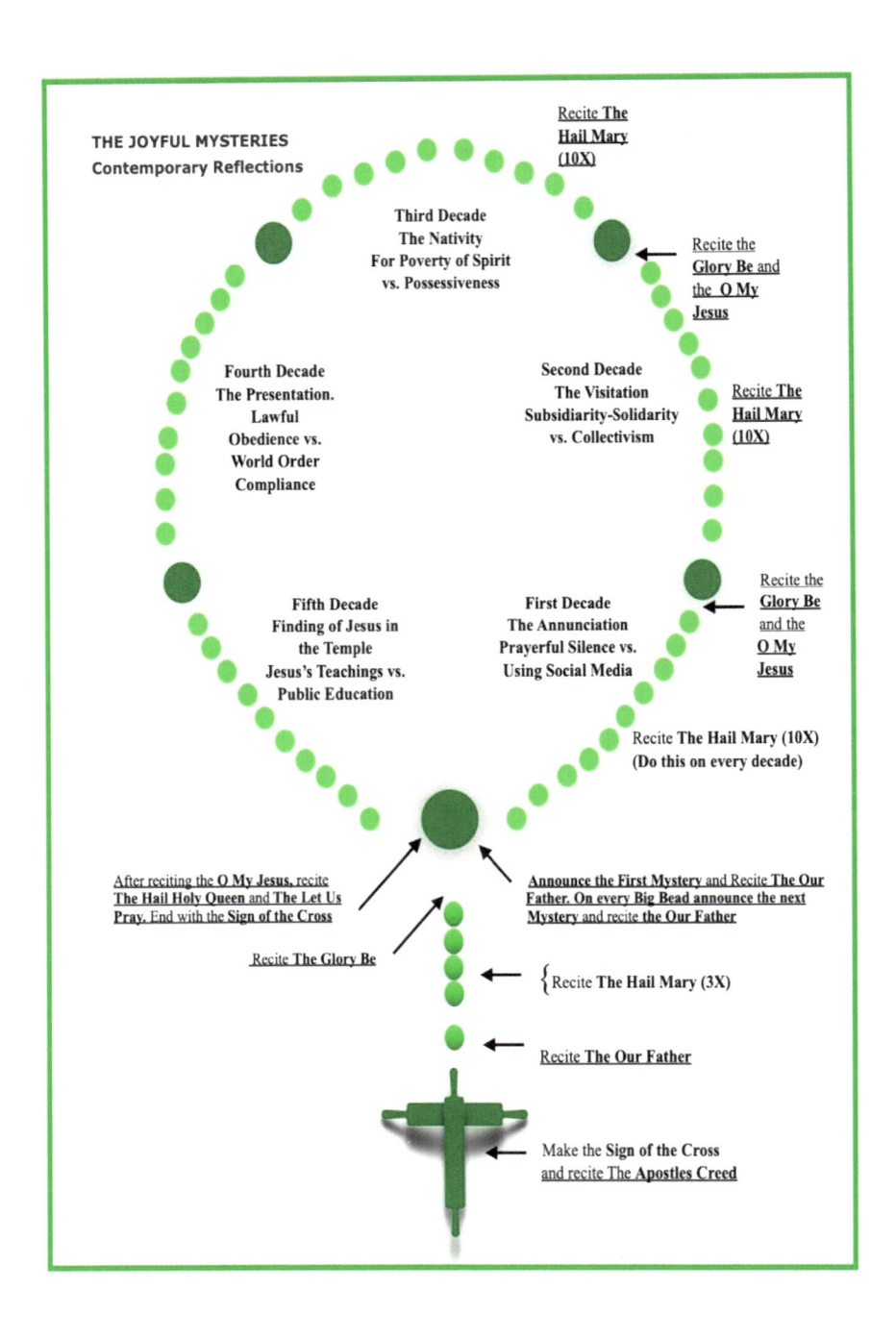

THE JOYFUL MYSTERIES
Contemporary Reflections

Third Decade
The Nativity
For Poverty of Spirit vs. Possessiveness

Recite **The Hail Mary (10X)**

Recite the **Glory Be** and the **O My Jesus**

Fourth Decade
The Presentation.
Lawful Obedience vs.
World Order Compliance

Second Decade
The Visitation
Subsidiarity-Solidarity vs. Collectivism

Recite **The Hail Mary (10X)**

Fifth Decade
Finding of Jesus in the Temple
Jesus's Teachings vs. Public Education

First Decade
The Annunciation
Prayerful Silence vs. Using Social Media

Recite the **Glory Be** and the **O My Jesus**

Recite **The Hail Mary (10X)**
(Do this on every decade)

After reciting the **O My Jesus**, recite **The Hail Holy Queen** and **The Let Us Pray**. End with the **Sign of the Cross**

Announce the First Mystery and Recite **The Our Father**. On every Big Bead announce the next Mystery and recite the **Our Father**

Recite **The Glory Be**

{ Recite **The Hail Mary (3X)**

Recite **The Our Father**

Make the **Sign of the Cross** and recite The **Apostles Creed**

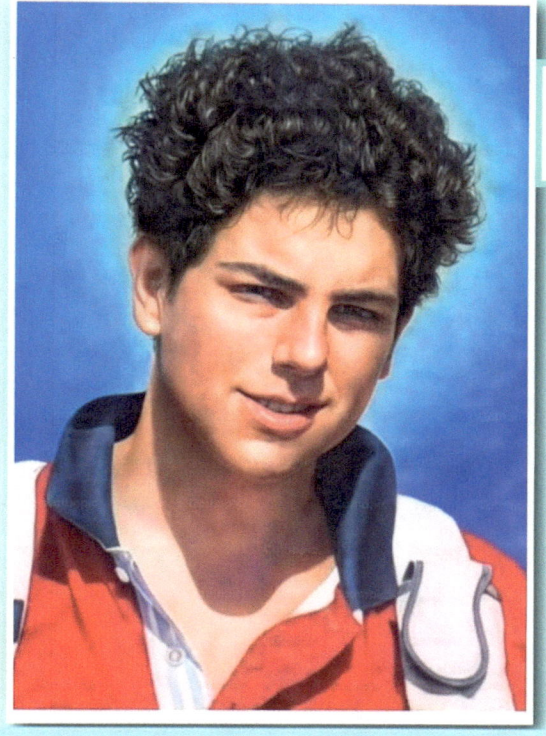

Section One - Joyful Temperance
Chapter One

"Mom, don't be afraid. Since Jesus became a man, death
has become the passage towards life, and we don't need to flee it.
Let us prepare ourselves
to experience something extraordinary in the eternal life."

Blessed Carlo Acutis
(1991-2006)
Leukemia took his earthly form from the created world.

THE JOYFUL MYSTERIES

Temperance

St. Augustine says: "To live well is nothing other than to love God with all one's heart, with all one's soul and with all one's efforts; from this it comes about that love is kept whole and uncorrupted (through temperance). Temperance is that which moderates and provides balance in the use of created goods. It ensures the will's mastery over instincts and keeps desires within the limits of what is honorable. (Paragraphs 1805, 1809, Catechism of the Catholic Church, noted as CCC going forward, Second Edition). In particular, humility reflects perfect temperance, as well as it being the foundation of prayer. (CCC 2559, 2628, 2717)

The First Joyful Mystery

The Annunciation (Luke 1: 26-38; John 1:14)

Virtue: Humility (devout silence, contemplation)

Snare: Pride (attachment to or superiority of position or opinion)

<u>Subject of Contemporary Reflection in God's Light</u>: ***Prayerful Silence vs. Social Media***

Intentionally striving to moderate "voice" in civic and church matters recognizes the risk of becoming overly distracted by worldly matters and even obsessive, rash, dogmatic, and temperamental or judgmental backlash. As Mother Mary silently contemplated Jesus in her womb, we should likewise strive to pray regularly before the Blessed Sacrament which will implant the seeds for any worthwhile communication. Intentionally, habitually replace vocal reactivity with a prayer before speaking or before writing on a social platform.

<u>Model Saint to Know and Imitate:</u> Given all the Divine surprises, twists and turns, St. Joseph, faithfully balanced his duties as foster father of the Messiah. Though no word of his is recorded in Scripture, by what is revealed we know he was a just and upright man. (CCC Glossary)

<u>Patti's Stumble Story</u>

Social media engagement can be the bane of humility. There are numerous anecdotes, so I will address this fault generally in two ways that have personally driven me…to sin and madness. One is what invades our senses if we permit it. Ever gaze through hooded eyelids at screaming anti-Christian public figures in the news or celebrated on TV and seethe that they are given unfettered, public forums, while your own squeaky voice is stuck in a living room echo chamber? This continued to plague me until I invited in Mother Mary and St. Joseph in those moments. The second general personal stumble was how I responded, misusing my tongue and typing fingers. Sarcasm comes easy to me, and on more than a few occasions, I have been guilty of thinking myself clever or glib. I may have scored some points with some, but at what expense to the souls of the person who latched on to my style or those I was deriding? Whereas, the Mother of God, Mary, pondered, I pounced. The same was true—occasionally still-with my quick retorts—damage done. How easy it is to speak the talk, but not walk **the** walk, but more harmful it is to walk over persons in a self righteous manner. Moreover, the "cover" of being correct on an issue is never an occasion to attack any person no matter how infuriating that man or woman may be. Certainly, there are public figures who have earned the indignation of many Christians, but always, judgment must belong to God. We may demolish the position, or condemn an action or incident, but not the person(s). Better, we can provide thoughtful, constructive solutions. I would have done so much more if I had been silent. Robert Cardinal Sarah (with Nicolas Diat) in <u>The Power of Silence: Against the Dictatorship of Noise</u> makes the salient point that silence is the indispensable doorway to the Divine.

<u>Mary's Stumble Story</u>

Social media is a power tool used to engage in immediate communication with a diverse audience. But like all power tools, if not used properly or with temperance and care, it can spiritually harm the user of that tool. When I first joined a well known social media platform in 2020, the ability to 'speak my truth' online was exhilarating! Finally, there was a forum where I could share the feelings I had about moral and social issues. Yet, I was conveniently hiding behind a covert profile name which I created to protect my identity.

In 2023, in a moment of clarity after praying for about twenty minutes at my computer desk, I felt compelled (by the Holy Spirit?) to go back and read all my posts from when I first joined that platform. What I had written—which I thought was funny or clever or politically salient at that time—was not so clever after all. Let's just say I *did not make the world a more beautiful place when I was untamed and uncensored on social media! Alas, some may give up candy for Lent or fast at various time of the year, but after prayer and clarity I began fasting from social media. At first it was hard to let go of the allure of viewing and responding to a broad audience of socially hungry readers who took no prisoners in the online gladiator sport of unchecked communication. Now, after some time away from this provocative environment, I only go onto a few 'safe' platforms on a very limited basis. I was snared into the world of social media and the result of this ungodly tool for me was not temperance, but hubris-filled sin.*

Virtue Narrative

Some people glue themselves to news and social media like Twitter, Instagram, Facebook, and the like or "yak" on line; other's simply "do." Their actions speak so much more powerfully. St. Gianna Molla, the tenth of thirteen children, was a woman who devoted her time speaking to God and caring for children through her pediatric practice. She also gave generously to the Society of St. Vincent de Paul. Likely this mother of then three often spoke and wrote about the preciousness of life and the rightful vocation of medical professionals. These principles were on her mind and expressed. A most generous doctor, she once aptly wrote—not on social media but—on a prescription pad, "so we doctors touch Jesus in the bodies of our patients: in the poor, the young, the old, and children."

Ultimately, she, too, would say "yes" to God and chose life for her unborn fourth child over her own self preservation. During the pregnancy of her fourth child (1961), in the second month, a tumor was discovered in her uterus. Gianna faced a critical decision: her life which she passionately cherished, or unknown, growing life in her womb. She did not hesitate…again with exemplary self forgetfulness, she proceeded with the pregnancy and clarified that if there was a choice between the two, she wanted her child to live. Though she survived surgery, and the child was born, St. Gianna died from septic peritonitis a week after child birth.

It was the pricelessness of her child and her absolute trust in God to take care of the family that is most remembered. Yes, St. Gianna "forgot herself," but God remembered. The world continues to celebrate and be buoyed by her holiness.

Gianna Molla's martyrdom became her eternal hashtag.

<u>A Contemporary Role Model for This Virtue: (Soon to be) St. Carlo Acutis, Cyber Apostle</u>

Carlo Acutis was an Italian website designer who used technology and social media to evangelize. His documentaries on Eucharistic miracles, his core theme, and approved Marian apparitions certainly obliterated the Dark Web with the Light of Faith. Born in London in 1991, the athletic youth lived only fifteen years until his death from leukemia, but what he achieved would be an everlasting tribute to the positive use of computers, as promoted by St. Pope John Paul II, one of Carlo's heroes.

He was noted for his cheery disposition and when he was bullied by other children in daycare once remarked that he could not retaliate because "Jesus would not be happy if I lost my temper." He gravitated towards adults and joined in praying the Rosary with a group of older women in the local Parish. However, he also helped the homeless and the destitute and attempted to imitate the life of a Franciscan. He loved animals.

In other ways, Carlo exhibited saintly virtues. A daily Mass attendee from a young age, he was nicknamed "God's Influencer." As a student, he was sensitive to those who lived in broken homes and defended young girls being sexually harassed by their male peers. He was instrumental in bringing his parents back to the Faith.

Carlo proved that mastery over self was possible even for the young most often tempted to succumb to passions and also mastered the excessive modern technology pitfalls.

CONVERSION STORY

<u>The Story of Dietrich von Hildebrand, Convert and The Soul of a Lion</u>

Dietrich von Hildebrand (1859-1977) lived during an era when the entire Jewish race was threatened with annihilation. Moreover, the roots of mass sterilization and abortion arose from this evil milieu to whole peoples via mass propaganda. While amazingly humble, Dietrich became the voice for those whose lives were being chillingly stilled by an atrocious regime. No doubt that he would have used social media (tech) for good, but one wonders if he would then have escaped Hitler and how much more Nazism and Communism would have succeeded then.

So humble a person, Dietrich von Hildebrand, staunch Hitler foe and remarkable Catholic convert philosopher, remains an obscure figure even among faithful Catholics. So, this conversion story expansively leads the others. In an outstanding *Crisis Magazine* article,

"A Portrait of Dietrich Von Hildebrand," Tom Howard creates a mini masterpiece of this Faith giant.

He underscores the timelessness of von Hildebrand's writings, but more than that, reading *Transformation in Christ, Your Path to Salvation*, highlights the incredible two virtues he embodied over his lifetime: humility and obedience. Pope Pius XII referred to him as "a 20th century doctor of the Church," and so he keeps company with other brilliant spokespersons for Truth but also the quieter souls, like St. Therese of Lisieux, for Divine Love.

For us poor souls striving to speak our souls against tyrannical political regimes of our time, Dietrich stands at the forefront leading us into that battle, showing how to do combat and not only preserve our souls but strengthen them. His temperate spirit well evaluated and wisely responded to intense threats but also fickle peers.

His life spanned many world changing events, shadowing the increasing rebellious spirit of the 19th Century through two world wars and the harbinger decades of internal revolution in millions of souls and eventually the Free World.

He was born in Florence in 1889, the same day as another great writer of history and the world, Christopher Dawson, and died in New York in 1977.

Two key influences keep alive this man's legacy. One, is his own works, but two, his wife, Alice von Hildebrand who noted his hidden grace. This once unbeliever in his youth had enjoyed even so the family acquaintances with figures of beauty, truth, and virtue. He studied philosophy under Max Scheler, among others, who reportedly formed the mind of St. Pope John Paul II. Dietrich von Hildebrand was baptized and received into the Roman Catholic Church in 1914, on the cusp of the first world war. This would have an indelible imprint on him, his view of a temporal world increasingly adrift from Faith and towards atheistic sadism that would kill millions in body and soul.

Eventually forced to flee Germany, Dietrich first went to Vienna but was sought personally by Hitler who condemned him to death. Austria eventually succumbed to Hitler, and Dietrich had a day's warning to flee. He lost nearly everything, surrendering his property in Germany which the Nazi's confiscated. Ultimately, he arrived in New York and was able to rebuild his family's middle class status.

Dietrich rebuilt while continuing his battle against Hitler though often meeting deaf ears. He taught philosophy at Fordham University for nearly twenty years and then continued writing in his private life. He would remain largely poor during his life and did not seek acclaim though it would eventually find him among the stalwart Catholic academia and faithful, attentive laity. Alice von Hildebrand may be greatly recognized for the latter.

Who knows how many this stellar convert personally converted to the Faith. Among other tidbits on Dietrich's life is that he reportedly emerged briefly from a coma and requested that the Te Deum be sung at his deathbed.

Rosary Intentions

Pray for virtuous self governance, in humility, that is well balanced with temperate public action. May the most vulnerable among us be spiritually guided to use technology for good and temper prayerful silence with moderation of social media....for self, spouses or close friends; family; neighbors (including perceived enemies or doubters); clergy and religious; educators; health care workers; business persons (including attorneys); politicians (elected, appointed, and government employees); and public figures including communicators and entertainers.

Section One: Joyful Temperance—Chapter One

THE JOYFUL MYSTERIES (Luke 1:26-28, 39-45; 2:1-20, 22-38, 41-52)

First Decade *The Annunciation: Set a guard over my mouth; keep watch over the door of my lips (Psalm 141:3)* **For: Prayerful Silence vs. Using Social Media.**

Add a personal faith quote or a prayer intention of your own at the end of this chapter to aid in your meditation:

_____
_____
_____
_____
_____
_____
_____
_____
_____
_____
_____
_____
_____
_____
_____
_____
_____
_____

*Helping ourselves and others to **FAITHFULLY** follow Jesus Christ.*

Section One - Joyful Temperance
Chapter Two

"You never know how much good you can do if you just try."

Blessed Julia Greeley
(c. 1833-1848-1918)

THE JOYFUL MYSTERIES

Temperance

Balance is needed when apportioning duties of the state with respect to the common good, and the principles of subsidiarity and solidarity are applied through Church teaching to best ensure just distribution for the needy but avoid excesses of government power. According to the Catechism, subsidiarity proclaims that the "...community of a higher order should not interfere with or substitute for the internal life of a lower order (individuals and intermediary bodies), depriving the latter of its functions, initiative and responsibilities, but rather should support it...always with a view to the common good." (CCC 1883) "Solidarity is an eminently Christian virtue" that promotes the sharing of material good, but, even more so, spiritual goods. (In Brief, CCC 1948). However, collectivism is opposed in all its forms as individual freedom is part of free will and one's responsibility for an action. (CCC 1734, 1735, 1738 and 1885)

The Second Joyful Mystery

The Visitation (Luke 1: 39-56)

Virtue: Caritas (Latin for "love"—translated into charity) for neighbor, including enemies. (Matthew 5: 43-48)

Snare: Excessive dependence on government to distribute goods and services in place of personal neighborliness with a tendency to distrust or discriminate against those whom we disagree with politically.

<u>Subject of Contemporary Reflection in God's Light</u>: **Subsidiarity-Solidarity vs. Collectivism**

True charity begins at home and then extends outward to other family members, neighborhoods, towns or cities, states, nations and the world in that order by the principle of subsidiarity and goal of solidarity. Genuine solidarity and subsidiarity are sharing the goods of the Earth and our Good God, in accordance with the Beatitudes.

Reject outright collectivism which diminishes the individual, squashes personal charity, suppresses reconciliation with neighbors, and enslaves people to tyrannical governments ruled by a few, atheistic elites.

<u>Model Saint to Know and Imitate</u>: St. Benedict Joseph Labre was born in the north of France in 1748. Although his father was a prosperous shopkeeper, St. Benedict Joseph Labre preferred the life of a pilgrim. He walked in tattered clothing but was rich in wisdom and charity. A patron saint for the mentally ill in our age, this "holy wayfarer" showed the world how love begins with self. At his funeral, numerous crowds streamed by St. Benedict Joseph Labre's body in homage to his personal touch in their lives. Accounts of 136 miracles were attributed to him.

Patti's Stumble Story

The old woman was bent over and obviously in need of assistance. I spontaneously approached her and offered to take her to lunch across the street at KFC. She gleefully accepted, and I felt good about myself. This self-satisfaction should have been my first clue that my "charity" was warped in some way. A few days later, this same elderly woman was in a small grocery store looking over the wares. This time, I hesitated. (This could become a habit.). Still, after wrestling with my conscience, I inquired if I could purchase something for her. The look that was cast my way seemed to convey that she knew I was reluctant, and she responded curtly, "No." I was rightfully contrite. I mused over my earlier outreach that had hardly dented my funds but pumped my ego. Then, I felt shame at the manner in which I had responded at the second encounter. A sense of duty is not giving; guilt is not a sign of loving giving. Thankfully, Our Lord granted me an opportunity for sincere atonement. Some weeks later, while walking from the store with bottles of ice water on a very hot day, I noticed her sitting on the bus bench. This time, I eagerly reached out with one of those bottles and was greeted with a broad smile. All of this was a valuable lesson for me. We cannot "count" charity on an abacus but must always be open to cheerful sharing. That does not mean we have to be imprudent, but the dignity of the recipient, that person, like an old friend, is always of paramount importance.

Mary's Stumble Story

Practicing charity is a sensitive balance when one is trying to compassionately understand every person's life situation. "Human virtues acquired by education, by deliberate acts, and by a perseverance ever-renewed in repeated efforts are purified and elevated by divine grace." (CCC 1810)

Only Jesus Christ can see into another's heart and truly know how that person's pain was formed and how it is manifested in outward actions. One day, as I was walking down the street in my city, I noticed a young man of about twenty-two sitting on the ground leaning up against a light pole. His hair and hands were dirty. The mother in me immediately worried he was hungry; I must feed him, I thought. I walked up to him and asked him if he would like a sandwich from the deli where I was heading to grab lunch. "Uhhh no..." he replied rather briskly. Then he asked me, "Do you have any money?" It was at that point I realized I was being asked to give him a different kind of charity: Cash. Was I willing to do that? Staring at him and taking in his direct request, I realized I wanted to give to him on my own terms. Not his terms. Could he sense that my 'charity' was deliberately conditional and possibly......judgmental?

"We ought to live sober, upright, and godly lives in this world." (CCC 1809) *This young man was not clear-minded and obviously homeless. Even so, I gave him money equal to the cost of a lunch meal. I did not want to look like a lukewarm neighbor. Did I feed an addiction instead of a human? What would Christ have done for this young man, I thought? Healed him? Said, "Follow me..." What I did was overtly clumsy and morally questionable. "It is right not to ...do anything that makes your brother stumble."* (CCC 1789)

Virtue Narrative

A story of charity and once peer of Dorothy Day: Father John McShane set up his altar for midnight Christmas Mass in the poorer section of West Las Vegas. [For information on Father John McShane see: https://www.reviewjournal.com/local/local-las-vegas/priest-has-spent decades-helping-needy-on-las-vegas-streets-1902736/] The temperature was near frigid, but as people shivered, he appeared unaffected. At one point he generously distributed warm socks to those poor mingled nearby. When, Fr. McShane ran out of supplies, he jumped in his car, drove to the store and bought more. Yet, this was only one example of the extraordinary love of this priest who some jested had put one million miles on his car traveling the state though he also oversaw a center hub for those in need in Las Vegas itself. Another story that circulated was the time Father McShane took off his shoes and gave the pair to a man without footwear.

Stories still abound about this 50-year career priest as he continues to drive 500 miles a week through Nevada and offer Mass and material assistance to the needy but also his devotion and commitment to the pro-life cause. Even when the temperature reaches 110, he might just mildly mention that he should remember to wear a hat. As spiritual advisor to Living Grace Homes in that region, Father McShane has been ever available to console and counsel women in crisis pregnancies. His love for the Eucharist knows no bounds, as well. If there was a living St. Francis, it is he though he currently performs his charity under the umbrella patronage of St. Benedict Joseph Labre Homeless Ministry.

A Contemporary Role Model for this Virtue: Sister Petra Palau Oviedo, Diocese of Dodge City, Kansas

In many places, individuals are making a difference, living lives of heroic self denial to serve persons in their communities. Sister Petra Palau Oviedo is one. Described by Catholic Extension as a nun "who lives out of a suitcase to extend the embrace of the Church," Sister Petra of the Mexico based Missionaries of the Charity of Mary Immaculate (MCMI Sisters) was called to serve the growing Kansas Hispanic community. With forty years of building up faith communities, the energetic nun immediately sought how best to meet the people where they were living. While her emphasis is on bringing the Church into their homes, Sister Petra is also building their understanding of what it entails to live out those teachings to best serve each other, their families, and communities.

To quote her: "Faith, hope and love, when shared, leave a faithful, grateful, and fruitful heart in the life of every Catholic." Thus, Sister Petra is building up the best of what is meant by subsidiarity and solidarity, family by family.

CONVERSION STORY

Denver's Angel of Charity: Julia Greeley

The canonization process has already begun in 2016 for Denver's Angel of Charity, Julia Greeley whose birth year is uncertain because she was born into slavery, in Hannibal Missouri, but it is projected between the 1830s and 1840s. Her early years were marked by all the hardships associated with this diabolical practice and made harsher by a cruel slave owner who was easily provoked with a whip. Once, as a small child, Julia's right eye caught the tip of the whip meant for her mother and was blinded. Later pictures of this most humble and loving woman show this mark of national shame. However, Julia was far more insightful than most when it came to knowing and embracing Jesus Christ, especially in others.

She was freed by the Emancipation Declaration in 1865 and came to Denver, Colorado around 1880.

Despite every reason to hate, Julia who possessed so little herself, always shared with others even to her own deprivation most often loaded in a little red wagon she pulled around. However, she shunned any attention and resorted to giving in the shades of darkness in alleyways to avoid any limelight and not to embarrass anyone, as she was a Black woman. She was even known to beg for others when she herself lacked resources. Indeed, she was a spiritual ancestor of Mother Teresa and a model figure for the Society of St. Vincent de Paul.

There was one treasure, though, that Julia craved, and ever sought, and that was the Body, Blood, Soul, and Divinity of Jesus Christ. She entered the Church at Sacred Heart Parish in Denver in 1880 and became an exemplary supporter of the Parish. The Jesuits there noted her extraordinary devotion to the Sacred Heart, and she often distributed literature to firemen, along her walking areas, as well as other Catholics and non Catholics.

A daily communicant, she later joined the Secular Franciscan Order in 1901 and remained an active member until her death in 1918. Hundreds of people passed her coffin, and she was laid to rest in Mt. Olivet Cemetery, but her mortal remains were transferred to Denver's Cathedral Basilica of the Immaculate Conception in 2017.

One extraordinary story about Julia was her encounter with a white couple who asked if she would help and mop their floors. She agreed and noted soon afterwards that this was a Catholic home. Julia inquired as to where their children were and the couple told the sad tale of their one child who had died. Julie foretold that they would have another child, and they did. The only recorded picture of Julia is holding that child who she called the little White Angel.

What greater tribute to Divine mercy and forgiveness, the greatest charitable acts of all that crowned her daily corporeal and spiritual works of mercy.

<u>Rosary Intentions</u>

As you mediate on this Joyful Mystery, pray ...for self, spouses or close friends; family; neighbors (including perceived enemies or doubters); clergy and religious; educators; health care workers; business persons (including attorneys); politicians (elected, appointed, and government employees); and public figures including communicators and entertainers *that they see Jesus Christ and themselves in every person and desire to provide for their needs as they would want for themselves.*

Concentrate on the true meaning of compassion which is to "suffer with" and for this decade of the rosary, consider one person who may need spiritual gifts for contrition, reconciliation, and conversion.

THE JOYFUL MYSTERIES (Luke 1:26-28, 39-45; 2:1-20, 22-38, 41-52)

Second Decade *The Visitation: For I was hungry and **you** gave me food, I was thirsty, and **you** gave me drink, I was a stranger and **you** welcomed me. (Matthew 25:35, author emphasis)* **For: Subsidiarity-Solidarity vs. Collectivism.**

Add a personal faith quote or a prayer intention of your own at the end of this chapter to aid in your meditation:

_____
_____
_____
_____
_____
_____
_____
_____
_____
_____
_____
_____
_____
_____
_____
_____
_____

*Helping ourselves and others to **FAITHFULLY** follow Jesus Christ.*

Section One - Joyful Temperance

Chapter Three

"True love is shown through actions, not just words."

Saint Vincent de Paul
(1581-1660)

THE JOYFUL MYSTERIES

Temperance

The Tenth Commandment forbids avarice arising from a passion for riches and their attendant power, and that this can engender other sins. (CCC In brief 2552; 1866.). People are often hindered in their pursuit of perfect charity by use of worldly things. (CCC 2544). More, envy is sadness at the sight of another's goods and the immoderate desire to have them for oneself. It is a capital sin. (CCC-In brief 2553). However, more important for our spiritual growth its to develop a "spirit of poverty," regardless of circumstances, good or bad. Spiritually, we have nothing without The Lord. (CCC 2546).

The Third Joyful Mystery

The Nativity (Luke 2: 1-14)

Virtue: Poverty of spirit that cultivates family sovereignty and builds society

Snare: Avarice (covetousness) that destroys family and society

Subject of Contemporary Reflection in God's Light: ***Spirit of Poverty vs. Possessiveness***

Blessed are the Poor in Spirit for theirs is the kingdom of God (Matthew 5:3) Poverty of spirit refers to the state of someone's soul, not an asset sheet. The materially wealthy can be extraordinary stewards of charity and, conversely, the materially poor can resent their deprivation. Possessiveness suffocates moderation and generosity.

<u>Model Saint to Know and Imitate</u>: St. Francis of Assisi was a model for St. Benedict Joseph Labre, and both were beggar saints. However, St. Francis has been misunderstood in our time, often portrayed as a "pacifist nature lover." While genuinely peaceful, St. Francis bore the stigmata and *in true charity* warned of the dangers of hell.

<u>Patti's Stumble Story</u>

In my twenties and early thirties, I subscribed to the "me" culture and was often angry with those I perceived were unfairly materially rewarded though mostly in my heart. The outside world might not have even detected that "thorn in my side," as I also believed in giving my time and talent to charity. Yet, I knew. I resented the boss who lived high on the hog while paying low wages; the neighbor who won a small lotto even though he was already financially stable; the flush landlord who sneered at our inability to pay the rent on time; the errant colleague who had ten times the purchasing power as I. And so forth. I was both poor materially and in spirit. So, I also tended to support political candidates who promised to equalize goods, compel higher wages and more benefits, and provide a government cushion. One might fairly say that I contributed only to the current state of affairs. The irony is that while I may be economically comfortable now, there is a certain discomfort in that, and the past has caught up. I now see the embitterment of others, as violent theft increases. The seeds that were planted by my generation have grown into a thorny bush. I pray for these poor souls forward.

Mary's Stumble Story

Personally, for me, the Gospel of the Beatitudes exemplifies the material poverty of Jesus juxtaposed against His true spiritual wealth comprised of mercy, pure love, and charity. Moreover, the 'love' of material things is not compatible with 'love' for the poor. (CCC 2445) For many decades I struggled with this concept. Envy of others who had more materially would drown out my logical understanding of Jesus's teachings: "Many who are first will be last, and many who are last will be first." (Matthew 19:30) In my blindspot, I was for years and years caught up in the manner in which our world ranks people by importance: power, popularity, and position in the community. I was much less influenced by how much my Faith would provide for my eternal place in Heaven—I was much more focused on the here and now: Me. Oh, ye of little faith I was. "Mary, Mary…" I hear my Lord speaking to me now.

Today, I am financially comfortable yet at what expense to my soul? Any earthly compliments or financial security I have attained will not buy a ticket to Heaven. Now I understand: "When her mother reproached her for caring for the poor and the sick at home, St. Rose of Lima said to her mother: 'When we serve the poor and the sick, we serve Jesus. We must not fail to help our neighbors, because in them we serve Jesus.'" (CCC 2449) Serve Jesus, first, not yourself: What would Jesus do? That's my first question to everything in the world now.

Virtue Narrative

Despite having many material possessions CP (Note: The actual identity of "CP" has been changed for respect of privacy) gives generously of his abilities, time, and wealth to help the poor and disadvantaged. CP, who is among a class often excoriated for being successful entrepreneurs and corporate leaders, has nevertheless never expressed any animosity towards those who seem bitter about his status but is a cheerful and determined steward.

Many have witnessed his genuine generosity in the United States and know he has gone south of the border to assist indigenous people bringing goods and building homes.

Furthermore, between his business work and personal sacrifice for Habitat for Humanity, serving the poor in foreign countries, and case management for the Society of St. Vincent de Paul, CP hardly has time for recreation. Still, he is the exemplar model for this Mystery and virtue, for it is not that anyone may be materially rich, but how that person uses those material gifts. If all the persons with money simply gave away everything, for the most part, it would be like killing the golden goose to theoretically obtain all the golden eggs.

A Contemporary Role Model for this Virtue: Mark Wahlberg

From contributing time, treasure, and talent to Tunnels to Towers Foundation for survivor families of fallen law enforcement and first responders, to praying in a church pew for Hallow, well known and popular actor Mark Wahlberg and restauranteur has become an exemplary example of living a spirit of poverty. Additionally, his youth foundation mission improves the quality of life for inner city youth through partnerships with other youth organizations by financial and community support. The 54-year-old father of four gives credit for any life success to his Catholic faith.

CONVERSION STORY

<u>A Story: From Humanistic Sharing to Heavenly Selflessness</u>

Dorothy Day was most famous for the 1930's Catholic Workers Movement, seeding numerous other groups, but her story did not begin with any consistent religious affiliation. Moreover, those who resent her conversion still attempt to pigeon hole her in more irreligious motivations and leanings to this day and towards contemporary "women's rights" and Marxism.

Although she was baptized in and occasionally attended an Episcopalian Church, Dorothy Day possessed no faith by her early adulthood years. Nonetheless, after surviving the 1906 San Francisco Earthquake, her family was forced to move to South Side Chicago where she learned about poverty first hand, at the same time simultaneously being spiritually enriched by a friend's mother, who was a devout Catholic. This unabashed woman inspired a burst of love in Dorothy that would later help kindle her entrance into the Church.

Dorothy focused on social work and used her writing ability to bring issues to the forefront of her day. Until her conversion, that script, despite being centered on the welfare of people, was always tinged with humanism and failed to embrace the individual dignity of each and every human being.

This extended to her moral challenges as she frequently failed in love, attempted suicide and underwent an abortion.

Still, like so many others, it was a child who pushed her to the Truth, this time in the life of her daughter, Lamar, who she decided to baptize in the Catholic faith which Dorothy had come to admire as the "Church of the Poor." Her embrace of Catholicism cost her standing with her former associates in the radical social reform movement, but grace sustained her and kept her focused on Our Blessed Virgin mother and many model saints like St. Francis of Assisi and St. Therese of Lisieux.

Among other trials, she was shot at while working for integration.

She prayed and fasted for peace at the Second Vatican Council and addressed the 1976 Eucharistic Congress in Philadelphia. She once remarked, "If I have achieved anything in my life, it is because I have not been embarrassed to talk about God."

In the end, she passed away among the poor in New York City on November 29, 1980, and a cause for her canonization continues.

<u>Rosary Intentions</u>

Pray for self, spouse or close friend, family, neighbor (including perceived enemies or doubters), clergy and religious, educators, health care workers, business persons (including attorneys), politicians (elected, appointed, government employees), and public figures (including communicators and entertainers) *that there is a renewal of seeking the good, true, and beautiful as the authentic treasures to accumulate in this world. Too, regardless of circumstances may generosity be shown joyfully.*

THE JOYFUL MYSTERIES (Luke 1:26-28, 39-45; 2:1-20, 22-38,41-52)

Third Decade *The Nativity: Blessed are the poor in spirit; the reign of God is theirs. (One of eight Beatitudes, Matthew 5-10)* **For Spirit of Poverty vs. Possessiveness.**

Add a personal faith quote or a prayer intention of your own at the end of this chapter to aid in your meditation:

_____
_____
_____
_____
_____
_____
_____
_____
_____
_____
_____
_____
_____
_____
_____
_____
_____
_____
_____

*Helping ourselves and others to **FAITHFULLY** follow Jesus Christ.*

Section One - Joyful Temperance

Chapter Four

"Prayer is the oxygen of the soul."

Saint Pio of Pietrelcina
(1887-1968)

THE JOYFUL MYSTERIES

Temperance

Oftentimes confusion about how to act or respond in a world gone mad can lead to inordinate and passionate responses. The temperate person listens to the Word of God, develops a well informed conscience as a light for his or her path, directs the sensitive appetites toward what is good and maintains a healthy discretion. (CCC 1783 and 1809). As this mystery also reminds of Mary's preparation for presenting Jesus in the Temple, how we present ourselves before God in purity, modesty and chastity also requires temperance (CCC 2521). In all, these virtues best prepare us to fulfill the duties of citizens. (CCC 2238-2240).

The Fourth Joyful Mystery

The Presentation (Luke 2: 22-38)

Virtue: Obedience (Listening)

Snare: Rebellion from lawful authority; Obstinance and Self Will

<u>Subject of Contemporary Reflection in God's Light</u>: **Universal Obedience to God's Law vs. World Compliance**

Since the time of Jesus Christ, people have been grasping at legal loopholes, but God does not change (Matthew 5:17-20). Still, modern times and technology have intensified worldwide rebellion against Truth to astonishing excesses. Never before have we so needed inspired "listening" ears. (CCC 2197-2200, the Fourth Commandment), wise counsel and prayer to save souls.

<u>Model Saint to Know and Imitate</u>: St. Padre Pio was an incredibly obedient servant of God. Many marveled at his acquiescence to higher authority even when he knew it unjust. Reportedly, he even counseled his traditional sister, a religious, to bear with her order which was becoming more liberal. As a good servant to God's Word, Padre Pio also loved and honored his parents until their death. In 1916, Padre Pio moved to our Lady of Grace Capuchin Friary located in San Giovanni Rotondo. This friary is located in the Gargano Mountains near the Adriatic coast. In 1938, Padre Pio had his elderly father, Grazio, come and live with him. It was reported that daily Padre Pio would personally feed his father meals and most certainly the Bread of Life.

<u>Patti's Stumble Story</u>

I opened yet another mailer during the 2020 election season that displayed a partially filled in absentee ballot application from a non government entity—Democrat leaning I learned only upon further research—that bluntly directed me to complete and submit the form. Moreover, clearly stated was that my reapplication was necessary if I wanted to vote in the run off. It was a lie! I was furious, composing letters to Georgia's Secretary of State, calling representatives, and griping with anyone who would listen. I received two more of these ballots if memory serves. Then there was the whole questioning of the election results.

How many times I have thought, "go off the grid"—live simply; do not pay taxes. How much I have fantasized sometimes that millions would "take down" what is left of those destroying an already crumbling Republic, though peacefully. Yet, at the heart of this emotional yo-yoing was a deep resentment about an increasingly tyrannical government. This was tough having been reared in a military family, expected to obey the law and respect government authority. As a teenager, I had babysat an FBI agent's children. A respected Secret Service agent lived across the street.

Yet, through the years, through the deteriorating systems of care, those in some position of "authority," from school administrators, to medical professionals, to local public departments, increasingly the onus is on the private citizen to simply comply. The COVID lockdowns that particularly targeted orthodox believers, especially Catholics tried the last nerve. Then I had to recollect myself as January 6 and the onslaught of similarly angered citizens began to froth at the mouth. I knew then, I could no longer take that worldly road. Slowly, I have rerouted my reasoning by the light of Faith.

<u>*How easy is it to forget in the heat of the moment that Jesus Christ, God Himself, submitted to the most brutal and unjust persecution in all history.*</u> *I purposefully look at the Sorrowful Face whenever I blank on that truth, and intentionally ask for signs of that redemptive realism. I also ask for the grace to pray for the souls of my worst "enemies."*

Mary's Stumble Story

When I was in my early twenties, the 1980s, the feminist movement caught my attention. A popular magazine called "Cosmopolitan" was a fashion magazine which not only flaunted the latest fashions from France and Italy, but hawkishly preyed upon young women like me to let go of my stiff moral compass and experiment with different social and moral concepts. I fell under the spell of choosing "freedom" through feminism and embracing organizations like Planned Parenthood who were eager to 'teach' young women how to make modern choices about their bodies in a patriarchal world. Birth control pills were handed out on a sliding fee scale. However, The Pill had its negative hormonal and chemical side effects. When I got into deeper moral trouble, this same organization was there to address my inconvenient truth (pregnancy) with a convenient solution: they advised me to 'discard' my situation as it was not a formed human but just a barely visible lump of indistinguishable cells at that point. Modern feminist compliance and my weak-will prevailed over adhering to God's moral authority and His will. It was then my soul was snared as I continued to believe the false claims of feminist doctrine over God's doctrine.

Why did I choose Planned Parenthood's pathway? I feared parental rejection which I had observed when my older sister, Donna, had become pregnant at eighteen and was sent away to a convent to have the baby in seclusion—given up for adoption. I also feared societal persecution. The man who had wanted to marry me during our five years of a monogamous relationship, emotionally stepped away from embracing our situation all together. And then desperate... alone...I fell flat on my face spiritually.

To this day, many confessions and spiritual retreats later, I still pray for God's mercy and for the souls of all the unborn children in the world and the mothers of those children who I pray will come back to God and see the error of their ways like I did. At one time in my young life, I traded off precious pieces of my soul to participate in a fool's gold errand of a feminist theory. The gift of finally understanding and discerning what real gold (the Way) looks like lifted me out of a dark and foreboding place. Only the Way, the Truth, and the Life can help people respond correctly and courageously to a confusing and contemporary Godless world.

Virtue Narrative

Today the challenge has intensified as Church leaders appear to be leading the flock astray. It is one thing to quietly ignore a priest celebrating Mass "commanding" that the attendees say "Our Mother" rather than "Our Father (true story), but another when confusion and vagueness emit from Rome. Thankfully, we have extraordinary models of obedience. St. Padre Pio is one such figure.

Incredibly, this holy man removed from the public eye, essentially silenced. Padre Pio could then only celebrate Holy Mass within the walls of the friary in the inner chapel. The public was denied access to Confession with him, as well, and he could not correspond with his spiritual children.

However, aside from forces within the Church, there were other trials for Padre Pio including the calumny that beset his reputation even in the area of chastity. Someone was always trying to catch him in some deception with secret listening devices planted around his domicile. Though justly defending his reputation, Padre Pio did not complain and submitted to his superiors in obedience from cooperating with any investigation that encompassed his stigmata to bearing solitude for several years. "God's will be done...The will of the superiors is the will of God." Padre Pio went so far as to chastise those who submitted petitions or wrote books, citing such behavior as disgusting, citing the supreme authority of the Church.

A Contemporary Role Model for this Virtue: Haley Robinson

An intemperate relationship—a slip in judgment—nearly caused Haley to lose her dream future, but it was also the overriding roundedness of her Faith which rescued her from further errors. Haley was anticipating graduate school when she tested herself for pregnancy. The positive result stunned the young lady who had been raised in a "good Catholic" home. How could she attend school, and where could she work. What would her boyfriend say. She recalls she "crumbled into a mess of fear and shame," never more scared in her whole life. However, she had always been pro-life, listened to the voice of her conscience, resolved to meet her fear head on, and drove to her parents. Barely breathing, their response would breathe back hope. Their wonderful loving response to the news uplifted Halley and carried her forward. (lifeteen.com)

However, Halley, ultimately listened to Truth and made the decision to inform her parents. She recalls she could not breathe the whole way home. The father of her child also "manned up" and took responsibility. In the end, her parents were Christ to her, and her son, Luke, was her light. By obeying God in the great trial, Halley learned that His Will, even when previously contradicted, can turn potential tragedy to victory.

Her story proves prayer works, and God reaches persons through many others. The world does not depend on any one of us, but it will be saved by our cooperation in truth and love.

CONVERSION STORY

Cardinal Arinze

Few may be aware of it, but the high ranking African in the Roman Catholic Church, Cardinal Francis Arinze, is a convert to the Faith, due wholly to Irish missionaries in his home village in Nigeria. The staunch supporter of the Magisterium noted in one interview for the *Irish Times*: "The school served in many ways. It made the children literate, and literacy opened many doors—political, cultural, economic, and religious." The Cardinal was hospitalized when he was nine, and despite objections from his father, he followed in the footsteps of a mentoring priest.

Yet, what many may not also know is that Cardinal Arinze is a pacifist, having seen the ravages of war in his own country. Moreover, he has made many inroads into other faiths, traveling in body, mind, and soul to no only bring the truth of Christ's love to all neighbors, but to listen to those whose beliefs are even contrary to the Catholic faith.

Certainly, one could imagine him at the stable when the three Wise Men approached the infant Jesus, and that he would have smiled at that encounter.

While some of Cardinal Arinze's work has brought criticism, he has journeyed forth steadily to embrace all God's children utilizing his gift for logic and his multilingual abilities to convert multitudes in largely Islamic and native religious regions. He speaks English, Italian, French, German, and Ibo fluently and understands Spanish and Latin.

Aside from his aversion to war which he concluded makes problems more acute, the Cardinal has also embraced the spirit of poverty and priests under his direction were admonished not to drive "fancy cars." Moreover, Cardinal Arinze is a steadfast apologist for the church's teachings and most notably outspoken against abortion and homosexuality. He ardently defends priestly celibacy as well. Many have witnessed his quiet but confidently firm allegiance to truth at one conference in 2018. During the writing of this book, it is surprising that Pope Francis has not called upon Cardinal Arinze to speak to the Israeli—Gaza conflict.

Cardinal Arinze epitomizes the good neighbor who brings news of glad tidings to all, respecting the dignity of each and every human being touting the peace that only the Sacred Heart of the Child Jesus in the Womb would impress upon the souls of those he encounters.

Rosary Intentions:

Pray for heroic obedience, listening to the Word and heeding the smallest letter of God's laws even when injustice is present and evil seems to be triumphing. Consider self, spouse or close friend, family, neighbors (including perceived enemies or doubters), clergy and religious, educators, health care workers, business persons (including attorneys), politicians (elected, appointed, government employees), and public figures (communicators and entertainers).

THE JOYFUL MYSTERIES (Luke 1:26-28, 39-45; 2:1-20, 22-38, 41-52)

Fourth Decade *The Presentation: For I take delight in the law of God, in my inner self. (Romans 7:22)* **For: Lawful Obedience vs. World Compliance.**

Add a personal faith quote or a prayer intention of your own at the end of this chapter to aid in your meditation:

_____
_____
_____
_____
_____
_____
_____
_____
_____
_____
_____
_____
_____
_____
_____
_____
_____
_____
_____

*Helping ourselves and others to **FAITHFULLY** follow Jesus Christ.*

Section One - Joyful Temperance

Chapter Five

"Faith lifts the soul, Hope supports it,
Experience says it must and
Love says...let it be!"

Saint Elizabeth Ann Seton
(1774-1821)
A wife and mother.

JOYFUL MYSTERIES

Temperance

The political community has a duty to honor the family, to assist it, and to ensure especially the freedom to establish family, have children, and bring them up in keeping with the family's moral and religious convictions. (CCC 2211). Elsewhere, the Catechism is clear that the state (civil society) under the exercise of authority (i.e. Department of Education) cannot command what is contrary to the dignity of persons and the natural law. (CCC 2235) Still, given our plurality, these expectations may conflict with those whose beliefs differ or even contradict Catholicism. Temperance primarily addresses the orientation of our passions, gnarly situations and temptations now arise in all spheres, but much affecting the faith formation of our children. There are numerous areas in the Catechism that help guide those in charge of our innocent children, primarily parents (CCC 1656-66, 1783-85, just to name some.)

The Fifth Joyful Mystery

The Finding of Jesus in the Temple (Luke 2: 41-52)

Virtue: Seeking Truth, Joyful Living, Holy Fear

Snare: Surrendering Parental Authority to Modernist Educators

Section One: Joyful Temperance—Chapter Five

<u>Subject of Contemporary Reflection in God's Light</u>: ***Jesus's Teaching vs. Public Education***

Perfect Knowledge and understanding are discovered in Jesus Christ, and wise persons will continuously school themselves to know, recognize, identify, and act upon truth. The well educated Christian, especially the gatekeepers, starting with parents (who are the ultimate guardians of the innocent) will also hone their temperaments to best counter the deadly forces now found in current government schools often indoctrination camps. Most importantly, they will form virtuous children in the Faith.

<u>Model Saint to Know and Imitate</u>: St. Elizabeth Ann Seton could well relate to the conflicts of modern society, as she faced challenges of being a widow, opposition from her Protestant family and an American culture hostile to Catholicism. Courageously she opened a school for children and pioneered many approaches. Yet her faith filled demeanor and persistence won over many in the public and clergy. It is upon her efforts that the spirit of Catholic schooling grew, and many children were able to avoid the snares of weaknesses in the public domain though the King's Bible was readily referenced.

<u>Patti's Stumble Story</u>

As a lapsed Catholic, I frequently simply walked past the nearby Catholic Church without a thought of the Blessed Sacrament. Then when walking my son to kindergarten, I was one street apart anyway. I admit relief that he was finally able to attend school, and, at first glance the teacher and classroom eased anxiety. The fact that it was a public school setting did not upset me in the least. What could happen in Kindergarten? (Little did I know, but then I was in darkness in those days.) For the most part, except for the school "losing" my son on the first day and an obviously manipulated PTA, the year passed well. More concerned about his academic gaps, I did not know though that my son would be "lost" in a different way before the age of seven. By the end of first grade, I knew public school, even then, was also in serious moral decline. Yet, worst of all, we—parents—at home had neglected catechesis and faith formation for our son for the first six years of his life. This was no minor failure, as this was a crucial formation time. Today, I am grateful for God's mercy that led him back but at great cost.

Mary's Stumble Story

When my children were in elementary school, I became aware that our California public education system was weaving many liberal social concepts into their curriculum. This egregious manipulation exposed my children to too much information at too young an age. Yet, the cost to pay for private school was well beyond my budget. Simply put: there was not enough money in my bank account to pay for yearly Catholic education when my two children were school age. I was working paycheck to paycheck with child support. The Catholic school closest to us was in another town and not richly equipped to help with financial aid to augment the cost of the tuition, either. The irony of that situation was painfully sad by the way. I'll admit I should have taken my daughter and son to church every Sunday. I didn't do that…I stumbled. Weekends were always a whirlwind filled with taking care of my kid needs and doing household chores. And, of course,

Monday mornings arrived much too quickly. This intense dynamic caused an imbalance in our family life which was palpable for my children. My children's father had moved out of town during our separation. Sadly, he did not move back to town after the divorce. The psychological and spiritual hurdles I found myself jumping over as a single parent weigh heavily on my psyche and soul. My children are very loved and their physical needs were always met, but, their childhood was serious and stressful.

From start to finish my children were raised in the public school system. Unfortunately, relying on the public school system to carefully shepherd a young flock properly is akin to allowing a wolf in sheep's clothing into my henhouse. And this is just what happened. Today, my adult children are deeply skeptical of any formal religion like many in their generation. Their view of finding faith in God has been replaced with a modern, secular worldview whose acceptance of religion has been savaged completely by agnostic or atheistic academic intervention disguising itself as "public education." As a person who was privately, spiritually comforted by God in my home, I also unintentionally contributed to their bias about formal religion whether it be Catholicism, Judaism, or any other formal religion. (CCC 2055)

<u>Virtue Narrative</u>

An Adorer: You will find this mother and teacher daily in the Blessed Sacrament Chapel in Eucharistic adoration, before or after attending daily Mass. For this narrative, we will call her Sophia. When one enters, she does not stir. If one watches her from a distance, her gaze never leaves the monstrance. Her lips might move slightly. Occasionally she jots notes in what appears to be a journal. Soon, she, herself, will be in a classroom with young children but will teach by more than textbooks. She will be a wealth of knowledge for these young minds, imitating Mary, the Seat of Wisdom, the first teacher of Jesus Christ. Her ten-minute devotions will cover the breadth of the school year. How wonderful for these fortunate youth who will receive a priceless education and most likely an exceptional academic one, as these are not mutually exclusive goals.

A Contemporary Role Model for this Virtue: Rosemary Vander Weele, M.A.

From the start, most evident is her love of the Catholic Faith tempered by an appreciation and grasp of sound education pedagogy. Though mostly reserved, she demonstrates extraordinary awareness when anyone is leaving the track of solid Catholic teaching, especially in various conferences and retreats, and express that alertness often silently but powerfully. A quiet departure from a disjointed lecture; a look; an unequivocal response to a parent or other educator quickly established the line over which she will never cross.

Today, Rosemary is a widely respected leader in classical education, particularly with the national Institute of Catholic Liberal Education (ICLE). Aside from overseeing two Denver Catholic schools, Rosemary is an acclaimed program leader and principal trainer. In her private life, she and her husband are joyfully rearing three children, and yet, she also managed to publish a small children's book.

The Catholic world of education is much brighter with Rosemary but also many others who are flocking to renew Catholic education in accordance with Church teachings and exemplarily mentors. Rosemary has inspired dozens of young teachers to follow her example, multiplying the number of genuinely qualified Catholic teachers.

CONVERSION STORY

From Fleeing the Truth to Finding Jesus in the Temple (literally)

No one facet of any human being can fully express that individual's full dimensions as a person. However, Clare Boothe Luce, noted journalist of the 20th century, embodied many different facets, and her early life, like so many other converts, significantly departed from any genuine spirituality.

As beautiful as she was clever, Clare came to the attention of prominent leaders early in life but also notoriously. Her first marriage to George Brokaw, an abusive alcoholic, resulted in the birth of her only child, Ann, but she divorced him in 1929. Clare plunged into editing and later sought success as a playwright. In the meantime, she also began an affair with Henry Luce, owner of *Time* Magazine and *Fortune* who was married at the time.

Eventually he divorced and the two married, but life proceeded tumultuously. After reporting on the war for *Life*, this multi-gifted vocal woman was elected to Congress in 1942. Then the tragedy of her life struck, and answers could not be found in human text of discourse.

Clare's eighteen year old daughter and Stanford University senior was killed in a car accident in 1944 while embarking on what appeared to be an upward trajectory like her mother. Likely Clare was impressed and proud of her daughter's academic accomplishments. By one account Clare spontaneously fled to a nearby Catholic Church. This began a two-year journey into the Catholic Church, aided by the late Archbishop Fulton Sheen. He reportedly "shepherded" her away from secularism and any links to communist thinking. She was later also confirmed in St. Patrick's Cathedral.

Her writing and oratorical dialogues shone with her fiery faith. She warned, "The yawning agnostics, the sneering finger-drumming atheists, the drooling, sentimental misty-eyed humanitarians…will not save us from the fiery sons of Marx." Actively anti-Castro (Cuba), Luce initiated a crusade against the revolutionary figure to whom she connected to Lee Harvey Oswald.

Four years after receiving the Presidential Medal of Freedom, she died of a brain tumor in 1987.

Rosary Intentions:

Pray for the wisdom of Catholic teachers but also the fullness of renewal of Catholic education for self, spouse or close friend, family, neighbors (including perceived enemies or doubters, clergy and religious, educators, health workers, business persons (including attorneys, politicians (elected, appointed government employees) public figures (communicators and entertainers).

Section One: Joyful Temperance—Chapter Five

THE JOYFUL MYSTERIES (Luke 1:26-28, 39-45; 2:1-20, 22-38, 41-52)

Fifth Decade *The Finding of Jesus in the Temple: As for you, do not be called Rabbi. You have but one teacher, and you are all brothers. (Matthew 23:8)* **For Jesus's Teachings vs. Public Education.**

Add a personal faith quote or a prayer intention of your own at the end of this chapter to aid in your meditation:

_____
_____
_____
_____
_____
_____
_____
_____
_____
_____
_____
_____
_____
_____
_____
_____
_____
_____

*Helping ourselves and others to **FAITHFULLY** follow Jesus Christ.*

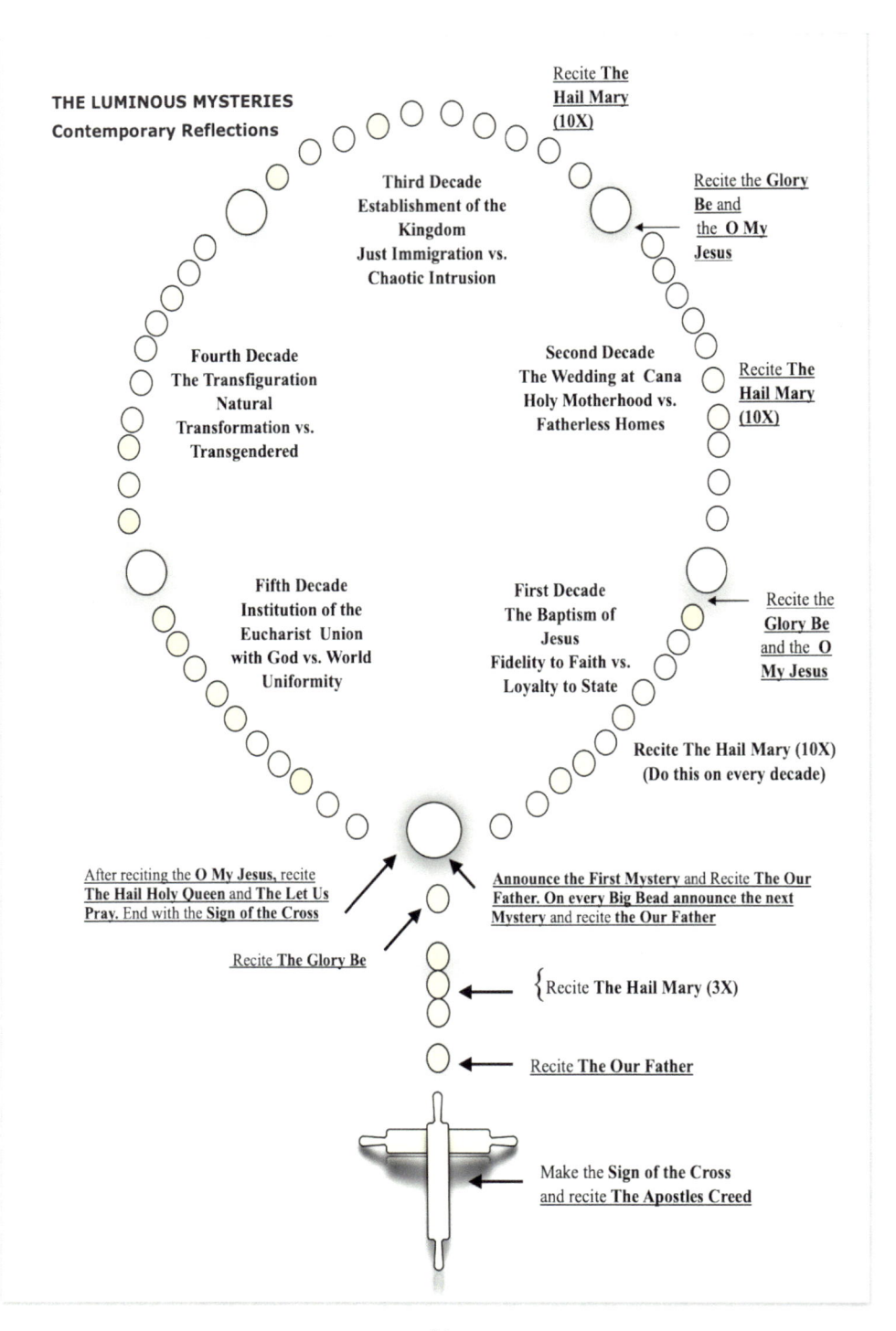

THE LUMINOUS MYSTERIES
Contemporary Reflections

Recite **The Hail Mary (10X)**

Third Decade
Establishment of the Kingdom
Just Immigration vs. Chaotic Intrusion

Recite the **Glory Be** and the **O My Jesus**

Fourth Decade
The Transfiguration
Natural Transformation vs. Transgendered

Second Decade
The Wedding at Cana
Holy Motherhood vs. Fatherless Homes

Recite **The Hail Mary (10X)**

Fifth Decade
Institution of the Eucharist Union with God vs. World Uniformity

First Decade
The Baptism of Jesus
Fidelity to Faith vs. Loyalty to State

Recite the **Glory Be** and the **O My Jesus**

Recite The Hail Mary (10X)
(Do this on every decade)

After reciting the **O My Jesus,** recite The Hail Holy Queen and The Let Us Pray. End with the **Sign of the Cross**

Announce the First Mystery and Recite The Our Father. On every Big Bead announce the next Mystery and recite the Our Father

Recite **The Glory Be**

{ Recite **The Hail Mary (3X)**

Recite **The Our Father**

Make the **Sign of the Cross** and recite **The Apostles Creed**

Section Two - Luminous Prudence

Chapter One

"A word or a smile is most often enough to put fresh life in a despondent soul."

Saint Therese of Lisieux
(1873-1897)

LUMINOUS MYSTERIES

Prudence may be the most critical virtue of our (any) era, and the illumination of each of these Luminous Mysteries conveys the necessity of wisdom so pointedly. It is also called the "auriga virtutum (the chariot of the virtues), guiding the others and setting rule and measure. Prudence "disposes practical reason to discern our true good in every circumstance and to choose the right means of achieving it." (CCC 1806). Prudence guides the conscience, especially for the baptized person who pursues a life of grace because the Cardinal virtues require human cooperation and effort. Moreover, the whole organism of the Christian's supernatural life has its roots in Baptism. (CCC 1810). Baptism is our passport to Heaven if we do not allow it to be defaced or expire.

The First Luminous Mystery

The Baptism of Jesus at the Jordan (Mark 1:9-11)

Virtue: Seeking Sacramental and Sanctifying Grace.

Snare: Denying Original Sin and Neglecting / Rejecting God's Gift of Grace

<u>Subject of Contemporary Reflection in God's Light</u>: **Fidelity to Faith vs. Loyalty to the State**

Baptism brings numerous graces to reason and act extraordinarily in ordinary life and to prioritize our citizenship in Heaven over a temporary residence here. Prudence from "providentia" meaning "seeing ahead, sagacity" also opens the soul to the Gift of Counsel, one of seven gifts of the Holy Spirit. Baptism seals us to Jesus Christ. The fidelity of the baptized is a primordial conditions for the proclamation of the Gospel and for the Church's mission in the world. (CCC 2044)

<u>Model Saint to Know and Imitate</u>: One might consider that St. John the Baptist, the last prophet of the Old Testament, was able to "look ahead" from the womb where it has been conjectured he was baptized upon encountering Jesus in Mary's womb. He was that "chariot voice" calling out, to make straight the path of the Lord who would proclaim the Kingdom of God.

<u>Patti's Stumble Story</u>

I ran on "empty" with respect to grace for at least twelve years straight. Politics and worldly affairs consumed my free time as I returned to old habits and sought to reform the world through human efforts and outcomes. I nearly threw out my true birthright trying to impress earthly powers. Today, I celebrate three days: the day of my conception roughly calculated to be in late July; my birth into the world; and my rebirth into the world to come in that salvation Sacrament of Baptism.

I was baptized on May 21st, one month after my birth. Sometimes, I stare at my Baptismal Certificate and wish I could revisit that day, as an adult. I definitely pray for the priest who baptized me. Maybe, someday, God will permit me to "see" that day and meet him. I know that absent Jesus Christ entering the world and taking on sin for me,

Original Sin washed away at His Baptism at the Jordan for all Baptized in water and the Spirit, I would be forever locked out from eternal life with God. So sad that I took that for granted but so grateful others prayed the outpouring of grace until I at last accepted it. Contrition, Confession, Penance and Repentance (spiritual CPR) literally revived the health of my soul. It fully struck one morning when I could barely think "Good morning, God" after a night of drinking. Miraculously lifted of that temptation even to this day, again, I know it was possible only through intercessory prayer and the saints especially Padre Pio.

It is also why I insist with everyone that they never give up on any person no matter how disliked or sinful. The Baptism at the Jordan was for all God's children! Recall the Good Thief.

So picture my absolute joy when I was asked to be godparents to two grandchildren. I can only pray that they, in turn, strive to live holy lives, and even if they stumble, seek the cleansing waters of Reconciliation.

<u>Mary's Stumble Story</u>

St. Thomas Aquinas once said, "Age of the body does not determine age of the soul. Even in childhood man can attain spiritual maturity." (CCC 1308) Is it not interesting that after my baptism I was in my most graceful state spiritually? And yet, what at such a young age of life did I know of this powerful grace? I was raised to believe in God and brought further into the faith by Catholic role models. Decades later, I squandered that grace, misunderstood my faith, took my faith for granted and was far less spiritually 'mature' in my twenties than the day I was baptized! My life had been a regression of grace after my baptism, not a progression.

I explored other religions to understand man's journey to God. Different cultures have different versions of a Messiah-like figure. Curious! It was not until I was in my forties that I began a mature relationship with Christ. I was asleep dreaming I was awake. My life was sheer folly and spiritual blindness. Coming back from moral recklessness, I realize how much the snares of evil are insidious and cunning in this created world. What prevented my growth and spiritual maturity? Temperament? Societal distractions? Lack of faith? All of the above. Yet, it was not as if God was not trying to reach me. Candidly, I also said, "Not now Lord….but soon." And knowing I was ignoring His pure love for me, He finally said in a most loving way in my almost fifth decade of life, "The time is now!" Cancer can do that to you. It's a wakeup call for one's conscience. The Lord rattled my cage and woke me up! Knowing what I know now, I would not waste one day, one hour, or one minute on anything that does not benefit the salvation of my soul, my family's and the whole world.

Virtue Narrative

In Acts 8:26-40, which relates the encounter between Philip and the Ethiopian Eunuch, Philip is led by an angel to head "south" on a particular road. There he meets the Ethiopian, a court official of the queen of the Ethiopians, in charge of her entire treasury. He is soon to possess a much greater treasury, though. The Ethiopian had come to Jerusalem to worship, was returning home, and was reflecting on the prophet Isaiah. God called Philip to approach him and soon learned that the Ethiopian needed assistance in interpreting this work. The humble Ethiopian replies to Philip's query about understanding of Isaiah, "How can I unless someone instructs me." Briefly contemplate this, as the Eunuch was certainly a man of keen intelligence and commanded a high post. Philip is inspired by the Holy Spirit, especially on the passage about Jesus Christ's Passion and Death and explains this to the Eunuch. Baptism is entering into the whole life of Jesus Christ including his passion and death. His words obviously touched the Eunuch' soul. Afterwards while traveling, they come to some water, and the Eunuch exclaims, "Look, there is water. What is to prevent my being baptized?" After being baptized, the Spirit of the Lord whisked away Philip, but the Eunuch continued rejoicing.

Again, here is a convert who does not "assume" anything, but proceeds with confidence to attain his salvation. Imagine if all of us were so inclined to evangelize, especially when prompted. We can depend on the Holy Spirit to provide the wording and direction.

A Contemporary Role Model for this Virtue: Patricia Heaton

Numerous baptized Catholics left the Church, but they found their way back likely due in no small part to prayers of others. These intercessors may be known, such as those in the family or circle of friends; others may be strangers that we will encounter in heaven. Some are saints in heaven. Known as reverts, these returned Catholics are growing in number and voice, though, and that includes public figures, or celebrities.

One such is Patricia Heaton, an exceptionally successful comedic actress whose dry humored TV wife roles belied the secrets of her childhood and marital and spiritual struggles she experienced in her private life. When her first marriage crumbled, much came to the surface, but not before Heaton found herself at odds with the Catholic Church. When she remarried, this mother of four felt without a church home but remained a committed Christian. Determined to find a close relationship with God, she embarked on a trek through "Protestant Wilderness".

In retrospect, Heaton later admitted that those difficult periods of her life may have been initially triggered at twelve years of age when her very devout Catholic mother died of an aneurysm that resulted in depression and thoughts of suicide. For years, off screen, her real life adult relations did not include frequent laugh tracks with men or the Church. However, the real change for her came when she realized that acting had become an idol.

An Opus Dei priest helped Heaton back to the Church and the true Faith. This led to having her first marriage annulled and the second marriage convalidated. In other ways, Heaton has blossomed as a courageous and committed Catholic. A long time, outspoken pro-life advocate, Patricia Heaton, also addresses other family related issues in the context of the Faith but with a down to earth simplicity and humor.

As witty off screen as on—who does not love her roles in *Everybody Loves Raymond* and *The Middle*—she once noted on social media: "Spent Mass internally grumbling about the lame sermon, received Eucharist, knelt down, burst into tears. (#NoOneExpectstheHolySpirit.)

No doubt that this remarkable return and growth was due to Heaton's deceased mother and other Catholic family members, living and deceased, who were instrumental in begging grace for this vivacious Catholic woman. This most likely included her sibling, a

Sister of the Dominican Sisters of Nashville. A story for another time.

CONVERSION STORY

<u>A Story: From the One to All Things New in One Child of God</u>

When one sees John Wayne on the screen, even today, one is truck by the raw, worldly masculinity. However, according to his grandson, Father Munoz, who referred to him as "granddaddy" in one interview, this hulking cowboy star was much deeper than the public imagined. John Wayne had a spiritual side even from his youth although it did not fully grasp him until his Baptism into the Catholic faith just prior to his death in 1979.

Among the observations of Father Munoz is that his granddaddy knew right from wrong and was raised on solid Christian principles in a Biblical sense. John placed God, then family, and lastly country in priority and even wrote simplistic love letters to God. Yet, as his gruff exterior showed, he also was so busy that he did not tend to the matters of Church and religion, at least Sacramentally, until the twilight of his illness from lung cancer.

Moreover, this immense figure off screen as well as on was likely significantly influenced by his wife of twelve years, Josephine Saenz, with whom he had four children. According to Father Munoz, his grandmother "dragged" her husband to many Church events and fundraisers that likely opened John Wayne's eyes to the reality of the Church, spiritually.

His grandmother, Josephine, most likely provided John with the solidness and consistency of faith in that she never remarried until after his death in 1979.

Father Munoz also believes that had his famous grandfather lived longer, Hollywood would have tangibly witnessed his Catholic faith. The looming cowboy actor might have been a real force in Sin City where moral values have rapidly declined at an exponential rate over recent decades. However, one could envision "the Duke" also instilling hope and grinning as he led the charge for change…in faith.

Rosary Intentions

As you pray this Luminous Mystery, ask that yourself, spouse or close friend, family, neighbors (including perceived enemies or doubters), clergy and religious, teachers, health care workers, business persons (including attorneys), politicians (elected, appointed and government employees, and public figures (including communicators and entertainers) *seek or return to the Faith of their Baptism and grow as true members of the Body of Christ. As the world seems afire in sin, may they, in turn, bring the Light of Jesus Christ to others.*

THE LUMINOUS MYSTERIES (John 1:19-28; 2:1-12; 3:31-36; Mark 9:2-8; John: 6)

First Decade *The Baptism of Jesus:* *You will love the Lord your God with all your heart and with all your soul, and with all your mind (the first and greatest Commandment, Matthew 22:36)* **For: Fidelity to Faith vs. Loyalty to the State.**

Add a personal faith quote or a prayer intention of your own at the end of this chapter to aid in your meditation:

_____
_____
_____
_____
_____
_____
_____
_____
_____
_____
_____
_____
_____
_____
_____
_____
_____
_____
_____

*Helping ourselves and others to **FAITHFULLY** follow Jesus Christ.*

Section Two-Luminous Prudence
Chapter Two

"We must…accept generously
the will of God, whatever that
may be, since that is
always what is best for us."
Saint Zelie Martin

Saint Louis Martin (1823-1894)
Saint "Zélie" Martin (1831-1877)
A French Catholic couple and the parents of five nuns,
including Thérèse of Lisieux, a Carmelite
canonized by the Catholic Church in
1925, and her elder sister Léonie Martin,
a Visitation Sister declared
a Servant of God in 2015.

LUMINOUS MYSTERIES

The prudent know and understand that Christian life bears the mark of spousal love of Church and Christ (CCC 1617) with Christ as the Groom. Compatible with that realization and our dignity is yielding by faith with the full submission of intellect and will to God. In faith, that human intellect and will cooperate with divine grace (CCC 154) to attain the final "wedding feast of the Lamb." (CCC 1602)

The Second Luminous Mystery

The Wedding at Cana (John 2: 1-12)

Virtue: Holy Submission; Wise deference

Snare: Self Dependence; Rebellion

Subject of Contemporary Reflection in God's Light: ***Holy Motherhood vs. Fatherless Homes***

Marriage is an opportunity to overcome self absorption; egoism; pursuit of personal pleasure; and open to self giving. (CCC 1609) Moreover, it is only in Holy Matrimony that grace perfects the couples love and, by this, they help one another to attain holiness and welcome and educate their children. (CCC 1641). Mothers and fathers who live the Catholic Faith are best able to create a home whereby their children also grow in virtue in the security of that parentage. (CCC 223-225)

<u>Model Saint to Know and Imitate</u>: St. Louis Martin Zellie is rarely noted in the absence of his also sainted wife, "Zellie," who had first planned a celibate marriage. God had other plans to which they submitted with great reward but also tremendous suffering. They bore both with a great love of God.

<u>Patti's Stumble Story</u>

My first wedding, a civil affair, lacked any miracles except the "miracle" that I did not pass out at the dinner afterwards. There was ample wine and other alcoholic beverages. Sadly, I had sought the temporal approval of my relationship with my husband. How the world saw me was more important than how God was involved. Yet, it was worse, see Scripture ...from the beginning (Matthew: 19:4-6)—there was no divorce. I was not validly married for two reasons. One, my husband was divorced, after being married in the Church. Two, we were therefore in a secular union, not one of Holy Matrimony.

Yet, that was only the beginning of the worldly spin until a fateful encounter with a Sacramento legislative aide in the early 1980s. God permitted me to fall deeply into temporal views about marriage, particularly second marriages, in my role as a second wife and stepmother. This all culminated in association with various advocacy groups for divorced fathers, and, at one time, I was as much a soldier for that case as any. Two incidents would profoundly impact me. One was my attempt at a poem about divorce and the injustices against divorced men who found themselves without home or family. Now, I will quickly interject that there are many cases of devoted men whose wives have decided to leave. This was not the case, however, and candidly, our marriage was founded on mortal sin.

So, here I was composing this poem, and I had the nerve, the chutzpah (meaning audacity) to ask God to help me, as I was stuck on a line. At this juncture, I was returning to Faith but obviously still quite skewed in my thinking. After some pleading, He answered with a blistering: Oh, fickle heart which doused Truth's flame, pray dark soul be lit, ere kindling morrow's shame. (Note: These were not the exact words, but sums up the ominous message.) Stunned, I realized in a flash my pride and error. It would change the course of my activities going forward.

The other was when attempting to persuade politicians in Sacramento, a lost cause, still, I insisted with then Senator Roberti's (1980s) legislative assistant, that the current child support laws with draconian enforcement would likely encourage women to seek divorce. She responded, "What's wrong with that?" Or words to that effect. The light dawned, the lightening bolt struck, and I realized that I was a participant in evil, not because I fought these laws, but that I was combatting them for personal gain. Suddenly, the larger picture loomed over me, and I began to fight the battle from a different perspective even against my own self interests.

<u>Mary's Stumble Story</u>

For this story, I must first say: "…And forgive us our trespasses, as we forgive those who trespass against us." This statement binds the first half of forgiveness to the second half; meaning our petition to Our Lord for forgiveness will not be heard "unless we have first met a strict requirement." If you want forgiveness, you must first learn to forgive your brothers and sisters. That includes ex-husbands, too.

When I married in 1987 at the age of twenty-eight, I had a dependable career in healthcare. I had been living on my own for seven years. Privately, I was already a lapsed Catholic before we married in the church. Before the marriage....during our courtship....I was excited for my future with my fiancé; albeit some internal misgivings (gut feelings) which kept resurfacing during our one year mandatory Catholic engagement period. We did not live together before we married. Unable to discern the reasons for my fiancé's emotional nervousness about marital commitment versus maintaining his independence as a 'single male'...we proceeded with wedding plans. I remember before we married my father advised me that my fiancé was simply suffering from "bachelor's cold feet." I wanted to believe my father. However, my father was dying of cancer and not truly able to take in the full scope of my dilemma. Perhaps my guardian angel was trying to help me and I ignored his messages? Before and after we married, my husband was unable to overcome the snares of compulsions.

The Feminist Majority Foundation was founded between 1987 to 1989. I was a career women in the middle of this new movement; believed in the Feminist Majority Foundation's mission to create educational programs for women, address violence against women, provide health and job opportunities for women, and eliminate the sexual objectification of females by addressing pornography. I felt these initiatives on their face were morally sound and legally reasonable. Especially the deformed view of seeing woman as inferior or worse as sexual objects. I felt this was and still is a societal problem which destroys family life. The evils of pornography need to be crushed!

The feminist position which I formerly adopted pitted women against men in an unhealthy way. Through prayer and discernment, I now see that men are simply tools of Satan like woman can be tools.

I also have discerned that "Female Empowerment" was just Stage One of what was to eventually develop into what is now a disordered message which promotes outright female militancy—a rebellion against the sacred order of womanhood, motherhood, and traditional family life.

The civil dissolution of my marriage and the Catholic annulment was due in part to my inability to forgive his emotional fear of disclosing his moral issues during our engagement period and to forgive and pray for his ability to stop compulsions. That said, once we were married, and we had a child fairly quickly, we were faced with these snares which engulfed us. I pray for forgiveness and say: But for the sake of my children's upbringing, for the sake of keeping a marriage together and forgiving my spouse, for the sake of helping one another work through a spouses' transgressions so that a marriage can discover a deeper faith in God together... We fell AWAY from one another. We did not cleave together, but rather we lived self-righteously alone in our feelings instead of seeking God for mercy, comfort, and love.

Our divorce was unfortunate for my family in so many ways! In the end, accepting one's cross in life or helping a spouse to carry their cross until they can do so on their own is not demeaning. It's not settling for less, either. It is accepting marriage as a faithful submission to God and following Him by renouncing ourselves. I forgive my ex-spouse and I pray for him every day. He took financial responsibility for our children. What God has put together remains a designed creation of love which I see every day in the eyes of my daughter and my son whom I love with all my heart and soul.

Virtue Narrative

We can imagine the couple at Cana, as they must have been very special for Mary to approach her Son with the dilemma about the wine. However, this story is far more illuminating than a shortage of wine indicates and is no mere parable, but a true tale enacted with real persons. The Wedding at Cana is a luminous mystery because it required the very Light of Life to elevate marriage to the perfect union with God, stewardship opportunity, ushering in new life to give glory to the Creator, and a pre-announcement of the New Covenant. Of course, God knew that this wedding feast would be, but still the smooth manner in which the "best wine was saved for last" also predisposed that the couple were chosen for their anticipated cooperation with Divine Will in the unveiling of Jesus Christ's first public miracle, the nature of God's relationship with us, and prefigurement of his Passion.

A Contemporary Role Model for this Virtue: Dan and Stephanie Burke have been sharing the Faith as a devoted couple for many years. Founders of Avila Institute that offers courses and gatherings towards knowing and understanding truth, they also oversee or participate in several other endeavors promoting the same, including retreats. The most personable couple are also authors of many books and articles. These close parents of four children, one of whom works with them, and grandparents, they nonetheless have had their share of trials and sufferings. Both courageously and prayerfully faced the near death of Dan from COVID 19 in 2020 that landed him in ICU.

CONVERSION STORY

A Story: Chestnuts from Chesterton—truth in a nutshell

G.K. Chesterton, born in 1874, was a conservative Romanist (Roman Catholicism) well before his conversion to Catholicism in 1922. His droll sense of humor and ability to get to the point of a matter were two prominent facets of his personality that serve well today. One biographer noted that he once remarked, "A liberated woman is one who rises up and says to her men folk, 'I will not be dictated to' and proceeds to become a stenographer."

However, he also seemed to hold some controversial, if not contradictory viewpoints, including an idealistic notion about distribution of land providing each man with his own proverbial fig tree under which to sit. He did not provide a solid plan for such an ambitious endeavor, but maybe an idealist? Some even portrayed this classic writer and lecturer as anti banking and anti-capitalistic, but he was never an anarchist, and more likely it was the Gospel and his study of prominent saints that influenced his learning to ensuring everyone shared in a Christian way. Moreover, his scorn was mostly directed at the mega powers who greedily lorded over the people.

Among Chesterton's most acclaimed works are the biographies of two spiritual giants: *St. Francis of Assisi* and *St. Thomas Aquinas*. He also penned *Heretics* in which he took to task the great philosophers of his age with whom he vehemently disagreed: George Bernard Shaw, Rudyard Kipling, and H.G. Wells, though Shaw and Wells were personal friends. This was followed by *Orthodoxy* and *The Everlasting Man*, the latter of which is in two parts: "The Animal Called Man" and "The Man Called Christ." In this great work, G.K refutes the notion that Jesus Christ is just one more moral leader, or that Christianity is just one of many acceptable belief systems.

Among his more notable quotes are: "Fallacies do not cease to be fallacies because they become fashions." "It is not bigotry to be certain we are right; but it is bigotry to be unable to imagine how we might possibly have gone wrong." And…this classic: "The Bible tells us to love our neighbors, and also love our enemies, probably because they are generally the same people."

There is little wonder that Chesterton Academies are popping up nationwide. He is certainly a thinker to consult on today's world affairs.

Chesterton died on what would become the Feast of the Sacred Heart, June 14, 1936.

<u>Rosary Intentions</u>

Let us pray that ourselves, spouses or close friends, family, neighbors (including perceived enemies or doubters), clergy and religious, educators, health care workers, business persons (including attorneys), politicians (elected, appointed, government workers), and public figures (including communicators and entertainers) *seek wisdom of the Catholic Church in Holy Matrimony and the healthy formation of the family—or faithfully follow Jesus Christ in any vocational development and as the Catholic Catechism guides us.*

THE LUMINOUS MYSTERIES (John 1:19-28; 2:1-12; 3:31-36; Mark 9:2-8; John: 6)

Second Decade *The Wedding at Cana:* For whoever does the will of my Father in heaven is my brother and sister and mother. *(Matthew 12:50)* **For: Holy Motherhood vs. Fatherless Homes.**

Add a personal faith quote or a prayer intention of your own at the end of this chapter to aid in your meditation:

_____
_____
_____
_____
_____
_____
_____
_____
_____
_____
_____
_____
_____
_____
_____
_____
_____
_____

*Helping ourselves and others to **FAITHFULLY** follow Jesus Christ.*

Section Two - Luminous Prudence
Chapter Three

"Compassion is the language of the heart, and it speaks directly to the soul."

Saint Frances Xavier Cabrini
(Mother Cabrini)
(1850-1917)

LUMINOUS MYSTERIES

Prudently Catholic teaching does not address immigration so much as immigrants, stressing the dignity of individual migrants. Moreover, the Church has always stressed the importance of welcoming "aliens" and embracing persons seeking asylum and prosperity in a non-native land. In some ways, we are all migrants on a journey towards our eternal home, and it is upon that principle we should assess our spirit of welcoming strangers. The Catechism explicitly mentions the employment rights of immigrants in addition to citizens (CCC 2433) and the duties of public authorities towards foreigners, with some caveats. "More prosperous nations are obliged to the extent they are able, to welcome the foreigner in search of security and livelihood." Further, though, the immigrant also has duties: to respect with gratitude the material and spiritual heritage of the country reaching them, to obey its laws and to assist in carrying civic burdens. (CCC 2241; See also the CCC Section on the Fourth Commandment)

The Third Luminous Mystery

The Proclamation of the Kingdom (Matthew 6: 20-36)

Virtue: Holy Citizenship

Snare: Two Extremes: Hyperbolic Nationalism and Distain for Patriotism

Subject of Contemporary Reflection in God's Light: Just Immigration vs. Chaotic Intrusion

Sinful behavior, filtering through the political machine, has perverted the ideal principle of "welcoming the alien" by thwarting the development of just and dignified immigration. Through prayer, study of Scripture and the Magisterial teaching, such as reading about the Saints and seeking wise counsel, we could confidently advance the Kingdom of God. Ideally, there should be no "illegal" immigration. However, this requires individual prudence by both the native and the immigrant.

<u>Model Saint to Know and Imitate</u>: St. Frances Xavier Cabrini is considered the patron saint of immigrants and her example, prompted by Pope Leo XIII's request that she emigrate to America for the purpose of working with immigrants, still models for us how to treat the immigrant. Matters were so ugly and problems so compounded that New York's archbishop suggested she return to Italy. One wonders, though, how she would respond to today's immigrant population, much more hubristic with the threat of terrorism.

<u>Patti's Stumble Story</u>

Back in my breezy 20's, politics was the avenue of change. I trusted people more than God to improve the world even while I attended Mass on Sundays. I compartmentalized my activism in the world, but it often neglected the fine points of Church teaching. As such, almost every issue was scrutinized by a temporal lens rather than scrubbed by faith. Oh, I stuck to the basics about sex outside marriage, and guilt would plague me if I rationalized petty theft to cover a meal. However, on the bigger issues, I was mostly silent even when I would not consider making those choices myself, such as abortion or grand theft by friends. I eagerly joined the Democrat Party and was most open to such ideas as "open borders" then. After all, these were our neighbors, and Americans should share their wealth and good fortune—at least other Americans—because I was mostly poor in those days. I recall one incident when I openly embraced an illegal immigrant.

One of my roommates, who was often impulsive and naive, picked up a young stranger Mexican hitchhiker in his early twenties. He was quite friendly although he could not speak English well. In discussion with my friend, he disclosed that he wanted to meet American politicians so he could gather some student ideas for revolutionizing his country. It so happened that I was attending an event hosted by the famous San Francisco communist attorney Vincent Hallinan, who was running for a judgeship. So, off we went, and as we entered the crowded room, I spotted Hallinan near a fireplace. With a grin, I introduced the young man, not knowing if Hallinan spoke Spanish or even understood me as I quickly rattled off that the student was from Mexico and wanted to know about American politics for the purpose of a student revolution. Hallinan nodded and began speaking to this young man while I excused myself. In retrospect, I have no idea if anything fruitful came of that exchange, but not likely considering there were no forthcoming student rebellions in Mexico.

The student disappeared after that encounter, but I still have some fond memories of Hallinan though we would no longer agree about ideology. I admired the man for always being available to people, and he always did live his mottos, to the best of my knowledge.

I have since considered that I was unjust in a few ways, one being that today, I would probably suggest to this young man that he was wrong to enter here without due process and for purposes that were contrary to peaceful government transformation. We cannot pretend away the officious by smiles and hugs. While discretion in approach, words, and advice may vary depending on the individual, critical conversations must be achieved to save countries and souls.

Mary's Stumble Story

Most family history in America is based on our ancestors coming from another country by ship and beginning a new life here in America. This is how our great nation was built. In fact, my mother's Catholic Irish family and my father's Jewish Hungarian ancestors immigrated to America due to famine and religious persecution in their homelands. My ancestors were immigrants! They found gainful employment and became proud citizens of the United States of America.

Today, our immigration policies have caused me to become less than charitable about embracing "open borders" as a remedy to escaping "oppression." I am at odds with the Pope on this....forgive me as I stumble still! Embracing mass immigration without expecting an honest naturalization process or an efficient tract to citizenship is not sustainable for any nation. Firstly, it does a gross disservice to our immigrants who are suffering as it does not help them to understand our values and expectations as a nation. Secondly, it creates a victimhood which is belittling to the illegal immigrant. Thirdly, American citizens become collateral damage in the political immigration war in this country. Case in point: In 2001, I became a victim of identity fraud. My bank informed me that my social security number was associated with another woman's name on my credit history. The bank employee asked me if my name was also Maria R. (name changed for privacy) and if I was married to a man whose name I did not know. "No," I answered emphatically. I was told by the bank employee I needed to report this as identity fraud to the Social Security Administration and to all the credit bureaus immediately. Apparently, Maria R. used (bought illegally??) my social security number to a obtain a small loan, a gym membership, an account at a jewelry store, etc. Maria R. lived in Southern California. I have only ever resided in Northern California. What ensued from this personal violation was a two year nightmare for me to get my identity back as a citizen of my own country!

Improper immigration processes compel some immigrants to become criminals to get what they desire when they come to the United States. Conversely, immigrants who are good people, who want to work hard and become citizens, become stigmatized, too! It's grossly unfair. In the end, we are all victims of a broken and uncharitable immigration system which cries out for reform and justice. Let us offer a formal induction process to immigrants coming here. Let us provide immigrants a fair employer pathway to financial reward. And for those who wish to do us harm by coming here, let us be careful stewards and shepherds of our flock and protect our citizens whose families have already sacrificed so much over the decades to make this country a great nation. (CCC 2241)

Virtue Narrative

While we now view immigration through the lens of law, we have to admit that some immigrants, even those who illegally crossed the border in near desperation, deserve our empathy and assistance. Perhaps we should be thinking of St. Joseph, Mary, and the Child Jesus as they were forced to flee to Egypt. They were most certainly undesired foreigners, but God assisted them in every way, as noted by well known mystics. At the very least, some immigrants who sincerely cannot wait for documentation to ensure their and their families' survival may be "judged" by those virtues of Joseph, the preeminent patron of immigrants. By the Holy Family's example we can see that there are beautiful immigrants though sadly overshadowed, often in the media by hellions: ill intended, thieves, murderers and so forth.

So, this is a short story about beautiful migrants as witnessed by a devotee of Our Lady of Guadalupe at a special presentation in the early 1990s in California. But certainly, there are many more such stories to this day. The event was celebrating Our Lady of Guadalupe, and the devotee was gifted with an impressive print of that image for her prolife advocacy. Yet, what struck this devotee that day was not the supposed honor bestowed upon her for her advocacy work, but the look on the faces of several immigrants who were day laborers. Their weather-worn brown faces bore wide grins as they nearly bowed towards this devotee. The devotee later recounted that she was horrified. Did they not know she was hardly a model Catholic, let alone someone not "above" them? How could these obviously faithful "Joseph's" render her any attention, let alone a near-kneeling reverence which they extended toward her—a memory she does not exaggerate. She recalled that they had just reverenced the portrait and were completely devoted to Our Lady and life with deepest humility and without grimness or grudge. The women would often share this humble experience in the years ahead and as a glimpse into Heaven, where the just and merciful are welcomed and will reside together, forever.

A Contemporary Role Model for this Virtue: Kody W. Cooper

Kody W. Cooper, an Associate Professor of Political Science at the University of Tennessee, grasps the broader and finer challenges of the immigration crisis and within the context of Church teaching. Writing for Word on Fire (wordonfire.org), Dr. Cooper triggers thoughtful contemplation on this complex issue with an article titled, How Should Catholics Think About the Immigration Crisis? (April 16, 2024). Any sound role model will identify and address the twofold responsibility to both the host nation and the immigrant. It is the right of a person to emigrate, but the causation of such and how it is accomplished is a different matter and one subject to proper balancing. Moreover, no one should be compelled to leave their native land because of political pressure or neglect by that country in its duties towards its citizens.

Cooper also grasps that the host nation has a right to maintain its own distinctive culture, language, and traditions, which today are challenged by a significant number of immigrants including those who have entered the U.S. illegally.

He touts prudence—political prudence—as the principal virtue of legislators to determine the policies conducive to the common good. There are many facets to this issue that require wisdom and acknowledgment that poor public decisions can result in undesirable outcomes, such as child labor, sex trafficking, crime, drug trafficking and so forth. He points out: "The duty to love the stranger as oneself does not upend but rather flows from properly ordered love of self, family, community, etc." But Cooper also warns against Bible "proof texting"—or as we would call it "cut and paste"—as this is a dangerous application for making policy."

CONVERSION STORY

<u>Elizabeth Fox Genovese; A Story: Bound by the World; Freed to Proclaim the Word</u>

Born of a non practicing Jewish mother, Elizabeth Fox Genovese was a contemporary figure (1941-2007) that became transformed through self-reflection and an awakening understanding of the poorly formed secularized world around her. A controversial feminist, even when irreligious, Elizabeth nonetheless demonstrated the supernatural power of God's grace, akin to the miraculous Transfiguration whereby mere mortal man witnessed the absolute embedment of Grace in Our Lord Jesus Christ.

Fox Genovese attributed her political transformation from Marxism to a more traditional view of women, marriage, and family, to her then growing religious fervor. Although at one time a reserved supporter of abortion, she later acknowledged that it was murder. She also railed against many modern feminists whom she deemed as either too narrow in their scope of women's rights or off the mark completely.

Her view on immigration was also mixed as she opposed mass immigration as leading to exploitive conditions for laborers.

She converted in 1995.

Among other contributions, Elizabeth served on the advisory board for Women for Faith and Family and regularly contributed to its publication. In a special memoriam tribute by Women for Faith and Family, it was noted, "Betsy Fox Genovese will be long remembered for her intellectual integrity, her fidelity to truth, her fearless defense of all human life, and her courageous public witness to the Catholic Faith."

As an aside, hopefully the faithful women in St. Louis can regenerate Women for Faith and Family which was an outstanding and quite visible force for genuine femininity and the power of women in the 80s and 90s, particularly.

Like many intellectuals, Fox Genovese struggled with myriad issues and how to best address them even as she felt called to the Catholic Church. However, like many of us now engaged in our confusion about what to do given our incredibly poor choices of leadership, we might do well to recall her final analysis on the issue.

In *Caught in the Web of Grace*, she acknowledged: "The growing struggle in my heart and soul was not, however, a matter of left or right, but rather one of right and wrong and our ability to recognize them."

Rosary Intentions

Pray for a world united towards God and open, as nations, to those seeking a good life but well ordered spiritually, for self spouses close friend, family, neighbors (perceived enemies or doubters), clergy and religious, educators, health care workers, business persons (including attorneys), politicians (elected, appointed, government employees), and public figures (including communicators and entertainers) *and though in doubt or opposed to God seek the perfection of Heaven, not a brief peace or false utopia on Earth.*

THE LUMINOUS MYSTERIES (John 1:19-28; 2:1-12; 3:31-36; Mark 9:2-8; John: 6)

Third Decade *The Establishment of the Kingdom of God*: *The purpose of the law is to serve justice and mercy. (Matthew 23:23)* **For: Just Immigration vs. Chaotic Intrusion.**

Add a personal faith quote or a prayer intention of your own at the end of this chapter to aid in your meditation:

_____
_____
_____
_____
_____
_____
_____
_____
_____
_____
_____
_____
_____
_____
_____
_____
_____
_____
_____

*Helping ourselves and others to **FAITHFULLY** follow Jesus Christ.*

Speaking One's Soul

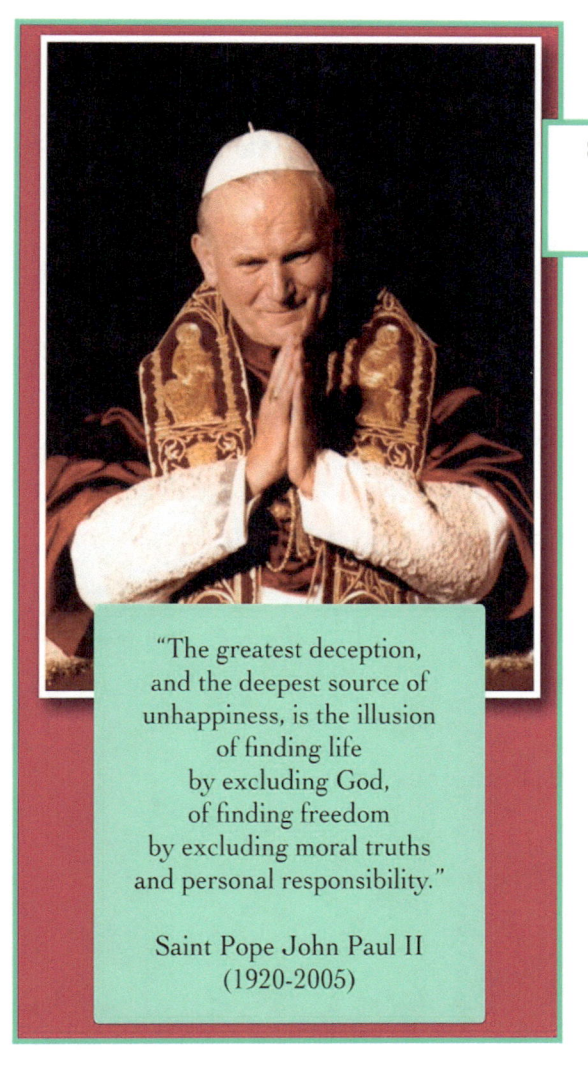

Section Two - Luminous Prudence
Chapter Four

"The greatest deception, and the deepest source of unhappiness, is the illusion of finding life by excluding God, of finding freedom by excluding moral truths and personal responsibility."

Saint Pope John Paul II
(1920-2005)

LUMINOUS MYSTERIES

Prudence is the ability to look ahead, and The Transfiguration gave some of the Apostles a window into the future, along with a foretaste of the Kingdom. Likely Peter, James, and John were selected to witness Jesus dazzling with light and experience the Holy Trinity on the mountain to fortify them when Jesus would be given up to a brutally cruel death on the Cross on a hill. Moreover, the disfigured, beaten Jesus would be restored to glory, His Body not only healed but magnificent in its eternal Being. (CCC 554-555). By this we, the faithful, are assured that our lowly bodies will also become like Jesus's though this comes about through many persecutions, carrying our crosses and following Him. (CCC 556) However, we must cooperate by respect for our own bodily integrity. Mutilation of any sort is against moral law. (CCC 2297)

The Fourth Luminous Mystery

The Transfiguration (Luke 9: 28-36)

Virtue: Transformation in Jesus Christ.

Snare: Ignorance or Rejection of the Theology of the Body

<u>Subject of Contemporary Reflection in God's Light</u>: ***Transformed vs. Transgendered***

Ridicule, rejection or significant mutilation of God's gift of corporeal being leads to physical, psychological and spiritual misery, especially for those who alter their sex identity or abuse their body. Though many are truly confused and need our acknowledgment and understanding, the world with the prompting of Satan has condoned and even celebrated a grave disorientation and mockery of God's creation. Furthermore, we are to give thanks for our bodies which the angels envy if for no other reason than we received the Body (Blood, Soul, and Divinity) of Jesus Christ in the Eucharist which also brings splendorous beauty to our souls.

<u>Model Saint to Know and Imitate</u>: St. Pope John Paul II, whose life was a continuous tribute to God of the gift of his own being, particularly his body which he also respected and treated well. He hiked and mountain climbed; acted; and constantly used his gifts to evangelize Jesus Christ, True God and True Man. Though, author of the sanctifying Theology of the Body, Pope John Paul II would soon be given an incredible cross to bear in the body. Yet, even when Parkinson's disease took away control over as his body, this servant of servants still gave thanks for life and welcomed the opportunity to suffer for Jesus. He gave an extraordinary example of how to die but with the firm hope of resurrection of the body and its subsequent glory that would be for eternity.

<u>Patti's Stumble Story</u>

I recall that evening in the college dorm suite when a group of us, male and female, decided it would be fun to play strip poker. Of course, alcohol flowed freely and served to lower the inhibitions though there was truly not anything particularly sexual about the game. In fact, my foggy recollection recalls how we even joked about the negative characteristics of our bodies. Yet, what is most amazing, when I think back, is not one of us even gave a thought about how we were abusing the dignity of our bodies by such reckless, ridiculing exposure.

At that point, I was still attending Mass, more of obligation than genuine faith, but it simply did not occur to me that what I participated in so willingly was ... wrong. A friend from that era still occasionally jokes about that memory. Still, it nags me that I was so blind, so far removed from the Real Presence of Jesus Christ, that my world then was almost exclusively earthly bodily fixated. Worse, I had deceived myself that I could be a faithful Catholic and engage in such folly.

As is typical of small foolish steps, left unresolved, in my later young adult years, I upset my body with contraceptives, and I am convinced that I almost died in childbirth because of the abuse. Artificial contraception is just that; chemicals not intended to bring health are dangerous and mutilating. I literally lost body organs because of that gradually over the years. If I could only make one comment to youth it would be to understand the theology of the body; cherish their being; protect themselves from insult and degradation, display the body only in graceful modesty when in the public, and engage sexually with a complementary sex in Holy Matrimony.

For how we regard our physical selves most often reflects how we are before God. Jesus Christ was transfigured in luminous Glory. He offers the same to us in Holy Communion, and that inner Light should also be clothed in graceful presentation, as well. Today, I am so grateful for that redemption and look forward to when I will be whole again in Heaven, as God created me.

Mary's Stumble Story

High school was an awkward time for me. I looked much too young for my age. Then came Senior Year—The Prom. I was not asked to go. So… to combat the awkward prom date girl-boy issue, the school administration encouraged the girls who were yet to be asked to the prom to put our names on a public list in the campus office. The boys could review the list and ask a girl who had not yet been invited. I put my name on the list at my parent's prompting. Two embarrassing weeks went by and no boy asked me to the prom. Argh!

Two years later I attended a college party—bumped into a guy who I had gone to high school with—a guy who never looked twice at me in the hallways or classroom at school. We chatted and I called him by his first name: Jim. Shocked, he looked at me and asked how I knew his name. I told him my name and reminded him we were in all four years of high school together! Stunned, he said, "Wow! Mary Sobel? Yes…I remember you now… huh… you've changed! You look NOTHING like you did in high school!! What happened to you?" I smiled weakly. Two years had made a real difference in my appearance apparently. Jim asked me out that night; he wanted to arrange a date very quickly. But…in a moment of fear, or mistrust, I stumbled over my words and clumsily declined a date. Rejected, he felt I was too curt and impolite to him, and he said so. Maybe I was. I did not feel his intentions were based upon who I was as Mary, the person. After all, why didn't he talk to me in high school when we had a few classes together? Where was my spiritual grace when I needed it? I gave Jim a snooty attitude because I was still immature and still discovering my womanliness. We never dated obviously.

Clearly, I was not yet comfortable in my hormonally transforming body. There was so much pressure to be physically involved with somebody. It is so easy for individuals to become snared or tempted into misusing their bodies due to a desire for attention, desire for unholy love, or a desire for peer popularity. These days it is encouraged by a liberal society to allow young people to physically disfigure their bodies, relieve emotional or physical awkwardness, or even disguise their gender by becoming walking billboards for disordered thinking. (CCC 2519)

Virtue Narrative

This obviously distraught young woman was looked upon with puzzlement. Call her Marie. She had just learned that her fiancé had betrayed her with another woman. Tears streamed down her face, as she gasped her disappointment and anger. How could he do this? They were both supposed to be virgins at the time they married. Now, Marie was broken.

The women in the room did not understand. This was college, away from the family, on their own, throwing out antiquated thinking, bowing to natural inclinations, and embracing the new "reality." This was the way with men. Did she not understand that? Men could …not … help themselves; sex was their natural drive. (Even the gay men in this circle joked about obscene scenes.) Basically, a coven of women sat there in the dorm room and tried to coax her into simply accepting that.

To her credit, Marie did not agree and broke off her engagement. What happened in her life after that is unknown; it was possibly better than her mockers. She had her dignity; respected her body and expected the same from a future spouse. Marie would not compromise on that.

Pray she found that noble man, someone who modeled himself after St. Joseph and strong Christian males. Hope that she enjoyed a happy family, one loyal to God, all children reared in truth and love. Also, hope she forgave her so-called friends' pride and sin in trying to push her towards what could have been a disastrous marriage. Finally, trust these women converted.

A Contemporary Role Model for this Virtue: Abigail Favale, Ph.D.

Abigail Favale, Ph.D., a professor at University of Norte Dame's McGrath Institute for Church Life, believes her personal and educational background has given her a keen position to assess the cultural climate surrounding gender studies, questions of gender, and creating a curriculum which offers a Catholic perspective on issues which pertain to sexuality.

Favale's faith journey began as a cradle evangelical Christian; different than the Catholic faith. Catholics value Church authority, traditions, and seven sacraments for grace. Evangelicals accept the ultimate authority of the scripture alone, recognizing only two symbolic ordinances: baptism and communion.

Following her Catholic conversion, in 2014, a significant shift occurred for Favale around the terminology and social attitudes around sexuality and gender. Favale's book, The Genesis of Gender, (Ignatius Press, 2022) presents the following: "A woman is the kind of human being whose body is organized around the potential to gestate life. This potentiality that belongs to a female is always present, even if there is some kind of condition, such as age or disease, that prevents that potential from being actualized. The very category of 'infertility' does not undermine this definition, but affirms it. A male human who cannot get pregnant is not deemed 'infertile' because he never had that potential in the first place."

As an evangelical Christian in her first year of college, Abigail Favale was dissatisfied with the notions of femininity and sexuality. In particular, the idea that the loss of a women's 'purity', once compromised, is lost. In this lost state, Favale offers, a woman can begin to experience low self-esteem and a damaged sense of dignity. As Favale delved deeper into the writings of the leading voices in the feminist movement during her academic journey, Favale increasingly questioned the core philosophy of the feminist movement. For example, if feminism means one must defend the removal of the age of female consent for sexual intimacy, Favale thought, how can the root of this philosophy bear good fruit? Moreover, how is the dignity of a young woman or a young girl protected if, by a lack of emotional maturity, a girl is unable to truly understand the consequences of sexual consent?

Even so, after receiving her doctorate, Favale focused her academic career in feminist and gender theory and considered herself a card-carrying feminist. Her experience of pregnancy and motherhood became the main catalyst for her spiritual conversion to Catholicism. During this time of her life, Favale came to the conclusion the feminist movement had very little to say about the sacred gift and loving acceptance of pregnancy, childbirth, or motherhood.

CONVERSION STORY

<u>Maria Von Trapp; A Story: The Hills Are Alive with the Sight of Our Lord</u>

Although baptized a Catholic, Maria (nee Kutschera) von Trapp, lost her parents at a very early age and was raised by a socialistic, anti-Catholic man appointed by the courts. By the time she reached 18 years of age, Maria was confounded and confused about her early life which she perceived was tomboyish and self-willed. In that state of puzzlement, she joined a convent, and reverted to the Faith and her sex by birth, and one might say, affirmed in Baptism.

While still a candidate for the novitiate, she was sent to be governess for the Baron Georg von Trapp, a decorated World War I hero and widower with seven children. Contrary to her own poor self image, the vivacious Maria soon captivated the family, and at the end of nine months instead of returning to the convent, the Baron asked her to marry him. By a special blessing from the Mother Abbess, and following serious soul searching, Maria accepted the proposals.

Together, they were blessed with one son, Johannes in 1939.

The family fell into financial ruin during the '30's, but it later became acclaimed for its musical talents and was the inspiration for *The Sound of Music*. World War II then took its toll on the ability of the family to perform together.

Aside from the robust family life inspired by the wonderfully wedded couple, the von Trapp's always expressed their deep faith in many ways. They sang together during religious festivals. Still, during their economic struggles their family home housed students and clergy. By special dispensation, even a room in their house was turned into a Chapel so Mass could be said. After relocating to the United States in the 1940's, the former home in Austria was transformed into a site for the missionaries of the Society of Precious Blood, "washing away" the stain of Nazi occupation.

Georg preceded Maria in death in 1947, and Maria died in 1987 at her resort home in Vermont. Their lives, though, exemplified the notion that sometimes, the best of our lives of Faith can be found on the mountain top, especially after trudging through the valleys.

Rosary Intentions

Let us pray that we are ordering well our lives with reasonable expectations, always growing in grace and as if we were citizens of Heaven visiting Earth. The includes gratitude for our bodies as God created them. Let us hope likewise for that growth in grace for ourselves, spouses or close friends, family, neighbors (including perceived enemies or doubters), clergy and religious, and entertainers). educators, health care workers, communicators, business persons (including attorneys, politicians (elected, appointed, government workers), public figures (including communicators

THE LUMINOUS MYSTERIES (John 1:19-28; 2:1-12; 3:31-36; Mark 9:2-8; John: 6)

Fourth Decade *The Transfiguration: And do not be conformed to this world, but be transformed by the renewing of your mind, so that you may prove what the will of God is, that which is good and acceptable and perfect. (Romans 12:2)* **For: Transformation vs. Transgendered.**

Add a personal faith quote or a prayer intention of your own at the end of this chapter to aid in your meditation:

_____
_____
_____
_____
_____
_____
_____
_____
_____
_____
_____
_____
_____
_____
_____
_____
_____

Helping ourselves and others to **FAITHFULLY** *follow Jesus Christ.*

Section Two - Luminous Prudence
Chapter Five

"He who wants to learn true humility should reflect upon the Passion of Jesus."

Saint Mary Faustina Kowalska
(1905-1938)

LUMINOUS MYSTERIES

Had any of the Old Testament prophets and holy men and women foresaw the Eucharist based on Old Testament revelation? Isaiah knew of the Suffering Servant, but what else might he have gleaned. Perhaps that was Wisdom beyond the Jewish leaders, but once the Eucharist was instituted, the Holy Spirit guided Christians to fuller comprehension. Dr. Brant Pitre's Jesus and the Jewish Roots of the Eucharist provides a fresh look at how the old was prefigurement to the new and was completed in the final Passover, the Last Supper. There are numerous other works that extol the greatest Gift ever given mankind in the Eucharist. However, the Catechism does establish its centrality to the Mass. (CCC 2177-2178). Prudent Catholics will seek not just Sunday Mass, as obligation but daily attendance when possible. The graces given to the soul fully contrite for even venial sin will illuminate the intellect, strengthen the will, tamp diversionary imagination, order the memory and temper the senses. It is the source and summit of our Faith (CCC 1322)

The Fifth Luminous Mystery

The Institution of the Holy Eucharist (Matthew 26: 26-30)

Virtue: Adoration of Blessed Sacrament

Snare: Indifference Towards or Desecration of the Blessed Sacrament

Section Two: Luminous Prudence—Chapter Five   111

<u>Subject of Contemporary Reflection in God's Light</u>: **Union with God vs. Worldly Conformity**

Fortunately, there is a renewal for The Eucharist and adorning the Real Presence of Jesus Christ in the Blessed Sacrament. Still, too many fail to recognize the priceless gift of even one Communion which provides the perfect union with God versus the eternal and devastating consequences for rejecting or desecrating the Host. One communion surpasses all superfluous friendships, obliterates all earthly receptions, and with proper disposition suffices for the suffering of a lifetime.

<u>Model Saint to Know and Imitate</u>: St. Faustina Kowalska of the Blessed Sacrament

The Diary of St. Faustina is replete with hundreds of references to Jesus Christ in the Blessed Sacrament in Exposition and Mass. Furthermore St. Faustina joined her suffering with the Passion of Jesus Christ in excruciating ways, but she also bore the everyday nuisances from people and situations, some minor but pervasive or chronic. She also endured the ridicule and rejection of a few fellow religious, some of whom gossiped maliciously about her.

Patti's Stumble Story

I was young but not ignorant. On a "dare" from fellow youth who I was obviously trying to impress, I wore a huge smiley face t-shirt to Mass and approached the Eucharist "under the influence." This mo-

ment is seared into my memory, and while I know it is forgiven, I cannot completely remove my silly, smug face (as I imagined it to have been) and the sense of audacity at my sacrilege. Years later, when I witnessed a young woman obviously acting out before and after receiving Communion, I asked, "Do you know Who you just received." I was not her superior but wished someone had tapped me on the shoulder or looked me into my face after my awful reception of the Person Who shed His Blood for me and asked that question.

Those related to this young lady irritably glanced at me. Perhaps I should have shared my own confession, but they quickly disappeared. I truly wished for that opportunity to stress I was not judging the young lady but only reminding her of this incredible miracle and God's perfect love for us. I can only hope and pray that our children are being taught better today about the awesomeness of receiving Our Savior.

Also, how grateful I am that I AM has welcomed and embraced me hundreds, if not thousands, of times since.

Mary's Stumble Story

For two decades I was not permitted to receive communion due to my divorce and my civil marriage to a spouse who was not spiritually ready to accept his Catholic faith again and be married in the church. I waited and prayed for both of us. I so hungered to receive the Holy Eucharist. This spiritual 'hunger' worsened year after year. I spent many years at Mass watching everyone else join in the Eucharist celebration. I observed others who appeared to take their communion privilege for granted; the many young people who would walk up to receive the Eucharist as if it was just a Sunday parental obligation. At *times I would weep seeing a particular young person, clearly bored, going up to communion. But more often I would weep for my spiritual desolation—a created self-imprisonment of my soul. (CCC 1332)*

Not until my husband was ready and we received permission to marry in the Catholic church, could I actively participate in communion again. During our convalidation ceremony, I finally received communion, received the Holy Eucharist. I almost fainted from sheer elation and sudden spiritual relief. I was immediately aware of His presence in me; a feeling I had not experienced EVER before in my life! It was if I was suddenly standing in Heaven, yet I knew I was in church.

To be away from Him while attending the Paschal banquet was truly an exiled experience. I would not wish that on my worst enemy! Where I have stumbled and fallen…oh how I pray you never have to walk that broken path, too. Thousands of times I prayed to the Blessed Mother and St. Joseph for the ability to come back to Him. They answered my prayers. Thank you, Blessed Mother and Saint Joseph.

<u>Virtue Narrative</u>

Like St. Faustina, St. Therese of Lisieux esteemed the Holy Eucharist as a priceless treasure which, in turn, led to her loving the very Sacred Heart of the Mystical Body and to communion of love for all persons. The example of her parents, also saints, inspired her at a very young age. They attended daily Mass and were frequent recipients of Holy Communion. Her sisters also gave great example, even eventually Leonie, as she struggled with growing in holiness.

Before her First Communion, Therese was participating in Eucharistic Processions, making many spiritual communions, and visiting the Blessed Sacrament in her free time. After an exceptionally joyful First Communion, Therese rarely missed an opportunity to receive Our Lord Jesus Christ. Sadly, the Jansenism heresy which rendered many people "too sinful" to receive Communion, including those who oversaw the distribution, such as Mother Superiors and priests, prevented her from daily reception.

Ironically the influenza pandemic of 1891-92 provided a consolation of receiving Holy Community daily. (What a tragic twist that our COVID-19 did the opposite!) Therese had surpassed the human desire, as well, and entered a divine quest. She focused on that union as a meeting of Heaven, and the world was simply an encounter with those she wanted to bring to the same upper rung of holiness.

For her, there was no other possession, position of power, or earthly persuasions that could deter her from the Eucharist, the Body, Blood, Soul, and Divinity of Jesus Christ.

St. Thomas Aquinas highlighted the theology of the Eucharist, but many afterwards often lived that love of the Body, Blood, Soul, and Divinity of Our Lord Jesus Christ.

Blessed Juliana of Mount Cornillon's work prompted the feast of the Body and Blood of Christ, known as Corpus Christi, and St. Margaret Mary Alacoque set the Catholic world on fire with her visions of Christ's heart in flames, burning for the love of mankind.

Another great embracer of the Eucharist was St. Ignatius of Loyola. When tempted to focus only on some Jesuits, turn to St. Ignatius for wisdom of discernment and peace of soul. He will be a saint for these times though we may not always detect his influence. St. Pius X was known as the "pope of the Eucharist."

Of all the Mysteries and certainly within the Luminous Mysteries, none is so wonderful for our immediate health than the Eucharist. All the events in the Life, Death, and Resurrection of Jesus

Christ are portrayed for us on a massive canvas. However, with the Eucharist, we become an interactive figure within that masterpiece.

In the Eucharist, if not in mortal sin, we receive the eternal kingdom if only for fifteen minutes or so. The Word is within us…the whole spectacular Truth rests in our conscience and in our consciousness. If ever in doubt, read about what the Saints declared through Church history or spend some time before the Blessed Sacrament.

<u>A Contemporary Role Model for this Virtue:</u>
<u>Colleen Carol Campbell</u>

Colleen Carol Campbell is not likely a household name, but then there are hundreds, if not thousands of role models for each virtue, many very close to us. They are not always found in Catholic sites, per se, but have ventured into the world to be shining light. Colleen is such, as she has made over 300 appearances in both mainstream media such as CNN, MSNBC and PBS, but also EWTN for seven years and Relevant Radio. An award winning author, some of her works include *My Sisters the Saints* and *The Heart of Perfection*. This wife and Mom of four relishes her quiet moments with God but has also managed to connect busy women and men with sources of spiritual wisdom and love of the Eucharist.

CONVERSION STORY

<u>Malcolm Muggeridge; A Story: From Earnest Atheism to Eucharistic Adoration</u>

Like many converts to Roman Catholicism, even in modern times, Malcolm Muggeridge traveled from socialistic atheism to Catholic conversion. His father was a member of the House of Commons in the early 1900's yet Malcolm chose the successful path of journalism and teaching replete with a controversial life of debauchery.

Among his works was his vivid account of the Ukrainian famine in the 1930's though he still persisted in an agnostic life style and wrote *The Earnest Atheist* in 1936. Later, after serving in the Army Intelligence Corps in World War II, he became a correspondent for the *Daily Telegram* in Washington and was briefly an editor for *Punch Magazine*, which often featured anti-Catholic caricatures in the 1950's.

Then, in the throes of the Sexual Revolution and social upheaval of the 1960's, Malcolm railed against the era's "pot and pills," became Christian and wrote the best seller: *Jesus Rediscovered*. This was followed by other works including his profile of seven spiritual thinkers from Augustine of Hippo to Fyodor Dostoevsky. His last book was *Conversion: The Spiritual Journey of a Twentieth Century Pilgrim*.

Eventually in this penchant for travel, Malcolm's affinity for India would eventually bring him full circle spiritually, when in his latter days, he met and was inspired by Mother Teresa to become Catholic eight years before his death in 1990.

Malcolm once wrote in *Jesus*: "Miracles are like modern day blood transfusions." If Jesus' miracles may thus be seen as a sort of spiritual equivalent of blood transfusion, in Malcolm's case it was not just a matter of dispensing a pint or so of surplus blood, and then having a cheerful cup of tea with a friend. Ultimately, on the Cross, Jesus gave all his blood, to the very last drop, not to revive one person for the remainder of a waning life, but to revive all mankind for ever; the outward and visible sign of this being the Eucharist, when Jesus's Blood in the form of the blessed Sacrament is offered to all who will accept it.

Rosary Intentions

Pray all persons cherish the priceless treasure of the Holy Eucharist as essential food: self spouse or close friend, family, neighbors (including perceived enemies or doubters), religious and clergy, educators, health care workers, business persons (including attorneys), politicians (elected, appointed, government workers, and public figures (including communicators and entertainers).

THE LUMINOUS MYSTERIES (John 1:19-28; 2:1-12; 3:31-36; Mark 9:2-8; John: 6)

Fifth Decade: *The Institution of the Eucharist: But whoever is united with the Lord is one with him in spirit. (1 Corinthians 6:17)*
For: Union with God vs. World Uniformity.

Add a personal faith quote or a prayer intention of your own at the end of this chapter to aid in your meditation:

_____
_____
_____
_____
_____
_____
_____
_____
_____
_____
_____
_____
_____
_____
_____
_____
_____
_____
_____
_____

*Helping ourselves and others to **FAITHFULLY** follow Jesus Christ.*

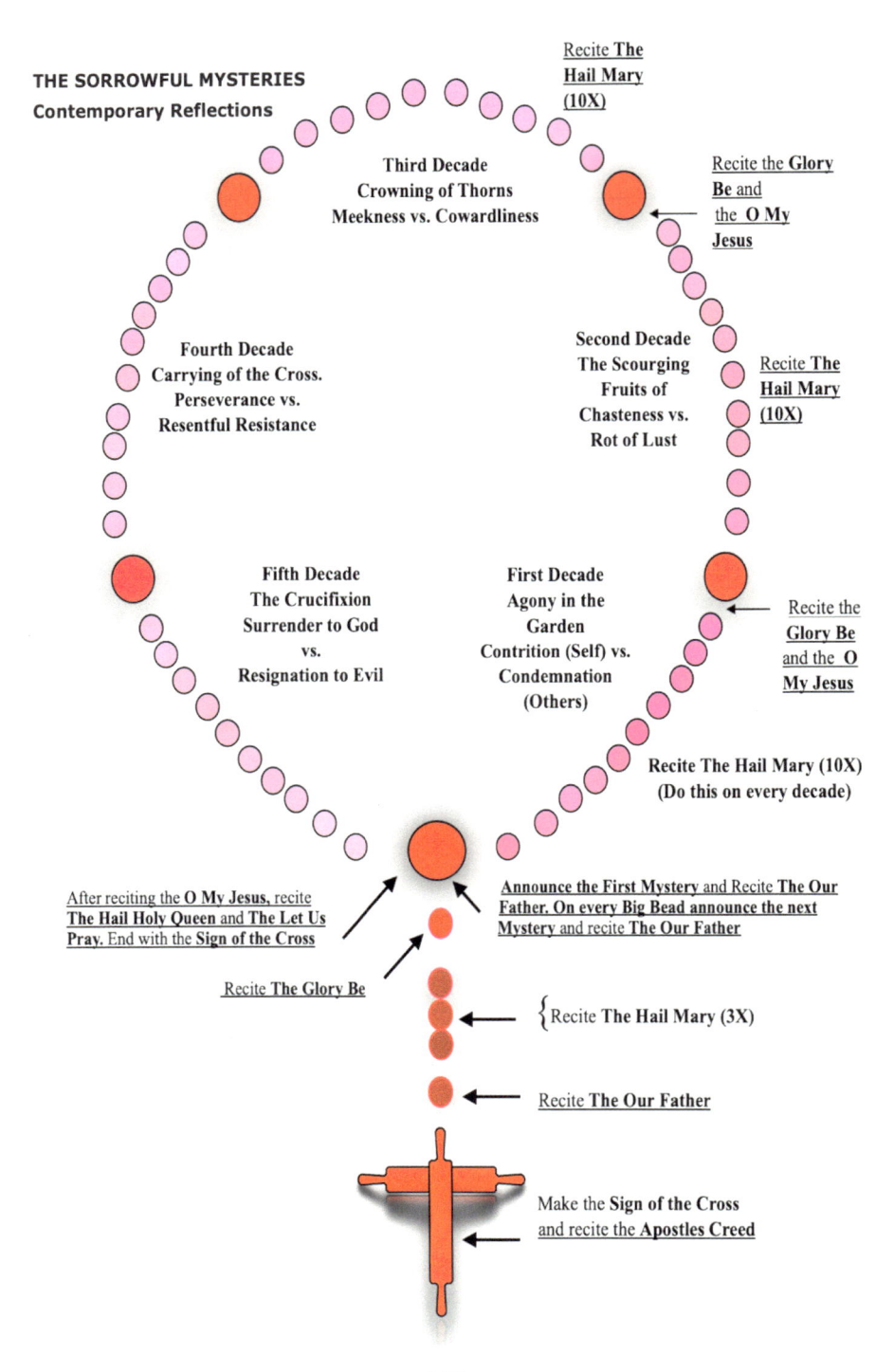

THE SORROWFUL MYSTERIES
Contemporary Reflections

Recite The Hail Mary (10X)

Third Decade
Crowning of Thorns
Meekness vs. Cowardliness

Recite the Glory Be and the O My Jesus

Fourth Decade
Carrying of the Cross.
Perseverance vs.
Resentful Resistance

Second Decade
The Scourging
Fruits of Chasteness vs.
Rot of Lust

Recite The Hail Mary (10X)

Fifth Decade
The Crucifixion
Surrender to God
vs.
Resignation to Evil

First Decade
Agony in the Garden
Contrition (Self) vs.
Condemnation (Others)

Recite the Glory Be and the O My Jesus

Recite The Hail Mary (10X)
(Do this on every decade)

After reciting the **O My Jesus**, recite **The Hail Holy Queen** and **The Let Us Pray.** End with the **Sign of the Cross**

Announce the First Mystery and Recite The Our Father. On every Big Bead announce the next Mystery and recite The Our Father

Recite **The Glory Be**

Recite **The Hail Mary (3X)**

Recite **The Our Father**

Make the **Sign of the Cross** and recite the **Apostles Creed**

Section Three - Sorrowful Fortitude
Chapter One

"I'll pray then as well.
Don't you remember
that Our Lady said I must
pray many Rosaries?"

Saint Francisco Marto
(1908-1918)
Victim of the 1918 Influenza

In the first apparition,
when Lucia asked if
Francisco would go to Heaven,
Our Lady replied:
"He will go there too,
but he must say many Rosaries."

SORROWFUL MYSTERIES

Fortitude

Fortitude, also often referenced as courage, ensures firmness in difficulties and constancy in the pursuit of the good. (CCC 1808) This gift of the Holy Spirit (CCC 1831) is the means to remain contrite and desiring to always do better and to sin no more; endure the scourging we deserve for all our sins, most particularly those against chastity; wear the crown of thorns that impresses on our arrogant brains that we owe all to God; carry our cross, no matter the weight, following Jesus Christ; and be crucified to and for the world, particularly those souls most in danger of hell. This is no easy task, and many great theologians and saints have underscored that such strength comes only through grace and may not be physical but also emotional and psychological. Furthermore, as Jesus reminded his Apostles, we must have the fortitude to die for our enemies, as well as our friends.

Family and friends may turn against us in myriad ways. Family may also become apathetic to our suffering, or life challenges, and choose to turn away from us rather than support us. Leaving us feeling like Jesus in Gethsemane when the Apostles continued to fall asleep instead of supporting Jesus in His suffering. Moreover, it may be easier to suffer for good people and causes, but when our very own betray us, how much that impales our hearts!

Also, fortitude must carry us on more than one isolated occasion, but daily, even by the minute. It is a cultivated virtue that has to be ready for exercise when the unexpected arises, as well. Indeed it is the armor forged by prudence under the banner of justice. Multitudes of souls have been saved by persons who face danger and death trusting in that Eternal City, but most importantly, guarding Truth in Love.

The First Sorrowful Mystery

The Agony in the Garden (Matthew 26:36-46)

Virtue: Genuine Contrition, accepting of penance

Snare: Spiritual Obstinance, Despair

<u>Subject of Contemporary Reflection in God's Light</u>: ***Contrition (self) vs. Condemnation (others)***

Courageously examining one's own conscience must precede critiquing a neighbor and ensuring that there is not obstinate blindness to one's own fault or rationalization of personal sin. True sorrow for sin recognizes gravity of sin and need for an honest confession but also mercy and forgiveness for neighbors, including those we perceive as foes. (CCC 1451-54)

<u>Model Saint to Know and Imitate</u>: St. Augustine, perhaps the most outstanding penitent in Church history, known for his classic, *Confessions*. This brilliant saint showed courage in both admitting his most previous life prior to conversion and in accepting God's gifts which included his incredible intelligence to lead millions to God and the one, Holy, Catholic and Apostolic Church.

Patti's Stumble Story

Growing up, we children were expected to walk weekly to our Parish church on Saturday for Confession. In those days, the church was often somewhat dark, the silence was ominous. Veiled women and hatless men, along with many youth, stood quietly in the lines that formed in front of the shielded confessionals. Some knelt in pews following their confession to satisfy their penance. There was an atmosphere of somberness fitting to the occasion. For myself, I must confess, either I did not pay attention in catechism classes or someone dropped the ball, but I did not do a credit worthy job of this spiritual task.

I generally covered my bases. How many times did I disobey? 300 should cover it. When it came to mortal sin, I could be scrupulous, and I do recall a time when the slightest offense could drive me to great anxiety and a compulsion to confess it. This was obviously in retrospect unhealthy and not a genuine reflection on actual sin.

Oh, I did commit mortal sins at times and was most grateful for that partition screen. Still, something was lacking.

In retrospect, it would have been wonderful to have had instruction on that Sacrament beyond the number, severity, and occasions of sin. Counsel would have placed the love of Jesus Christ more appropriately in my contemplation, along with emphasis on the grace we receive in this Sacrament. It was not until recently that Pocket Guide to the Sacrament of Reconciliation (Ascension Press) emphasized to me the desire for Jesus to forgive me. I also often suspect it was the shortcomings, for whatever reasons, in this instruction that led to the devaluation of the Sacrament to our present age when such is tragically dismissed all together. The either extreme, though, is worse than the former.

I am also absolutely convinced Padre Pio intervened in my life and saved my soul, especially around the time my father died. Both my parents were devotees of Padre Pio, and I began to slowly return to prayer when my father was ill with cancer, at first with just a decade of the Rosary.

At one point, when my father was given six months to live, I was strongly impressed with the idea that he should return to San Giovanni and enter the portal to Heaven there. I was so puzzled when, the doctors determined he had but six weeks...and then...six days. Then, my father, a career soldier and later passionate advocate for the developmentally disabled, passed from this world on Memorial Day, 1987, on the 100th anniversary of Padre Pio's birth.

My mother would die twenty years later on that same day.

It is unusual when I do not consider St. Padre Pio when preparing for Confession before or afterwards. However, he always leads to Jesus Christ who came to my rescue over thirty five years ago through Padre Pio and Divine Mercy.

Upon receiving the letter that would lead to the convalidation of our marriage I gazed at one treasured image of Jesus's face. Truly, the Glory was in His Sorrowful Face, and I experienced deep regret over my transgressions. Through the years, I have been graced with several fine confessors, but, foremost, I now know much better how to make that examination of conscience (should be daily) and access that Sacrament.

Mary's Stumble Story

Sometimes it felt as if my family were asleep and did not notice anything was wrong in my life; my marriage was failing and my heart was wounded. I wonder: Did I hide my marital despair out of sheer pride to keep my issues away from my family's view or did I hope they would see my sadness and offer emotional support? Probably both: Pride and self-pity. I felt my family subtly turn away from me when I became a divorced Catholic, (except for my mother who saw my suffering up close). In practice, I questioned my family's Catholic faith. In prayer over time, I was able to discern that my family did notice my marital pain and wounding. Yet, they were 'asleep' and, in that I mean, they were focused on living their own life. We were also siblings separated by geographic miles, as well. What also added to our sibling separateness? We were a military family that had moved frequently as my father served our nation diligently during his thirty year career. My siblings had their own states or countries in which they were born, which also contributed to an odd sense of separation from the lack of a consistent home life rooted in one family location. Also, my siblings were older. They were rightfully busy and focused on getting through their daily grinds, commitments, and obligations. Therefore, I turned to friends who became 'my family' in dark times. And whom still are my dearest friends even today. God bless them!

My initial condemnation (stumbling) of what I perceived as a lack of Christian charity in my own family of origin was simply arrogance on my part. (Matthew 19: 4-6) What did my family of origin have to do with any of that? Nothing. I was meant to suffer my sins alone....to despair in isolation and cry out to God in my own Garden of Gethsemane. To realize that His Will is the ultimate justice and His Will can provide the ultimate healing for my soul. For only He has ears to hear and eyes to see into my heart. In deep contrition and prayerful meditation with my Lord I came to realize that "whoever does the will of God is my brother, and sister, and mother." (Mark 3: 33-35)

His Mercy provided the gift of the Holy Spirit which helped me heal step by step—year by year. First came an understanding of my role in why my marriage failed. Then His counsel, fortitude to pursue constancy of mind and maintain clear thoughts, the knowledge of choices and human weaknesses. Finally, a fear of the Lord. This fear has led to full contrition….completely devoid of condemnation for anyone in my moments of deep prayer. Although I have made good confessions to priests over the years, face to face, and been absolved, I have had to learn to forgive myself—foremost! For I am His "beloved" and He showed me His merciful heart, during prayer, on more than two occasions. I will cherish the tangible gift the Lord gave to me which occurred on a Saturday, the eighteenth of March in 2023 (the feast day of St. Cyril of Jerusalem) until the day I die.

<u>Virtue Narrative</u>

This was a difficult choice: speak of St. Augustine and his Confessions or highlight St. Padre Pio. Then, we thought: What would a conversation between the two be like? Of course, they have already done this in Heaven.

We know that St. Augustine had a major impact on Padre Pio because both were so steeped in prayer, the breath of the soul. Moreover, Padre Pio converted souls at every opportunity. Even today, such enterprises as Padre Pio Press include "Spiritual Growth, St. Augustine on Prayer." From *St. Augustine Answers 101 Questions on Prayer* (a compilation from his many writings.)

Seeking and prayer led St. Augustine to truth, and St. Padre Pio's seeking of lost souls and his prayers led to many conversions. St. Padre Pio was a rare "soul reader" and could and did call out many sinners for their poor confessions, often either dismissing outright a false penitent (though some returned quite contrite) or cross examining the one confessing, eerily with a better "memory" of the person confessing. Stories abound in various books about these incidents. Joyfully, those today, can still be spiritual children of Padre Pio if they are willing to do the "work."

A Contemporary Role Model for this Virtue: (Two are selected here to provide a more 'global' perspective.). Rep Dan Lipinski D-Ill and Serge Abad Gallardo

Congressman Lipinski proves that one cannot broad brush an entire political party affiliation as Catholic friendly or anti-Catholic. Lipinski reputedly stood by Catholic beliefs including the right to life and did not abandon these even at the cost of his career. Yet, he also has lived his political life in ways that are not condemning of his associates but a light on Truth. Such a balance demonstrates the fruit of fortitude.

Increasingly, aside from America, we can also celebrate the many returning to the Catholic faith outside the country. Among them are the aspiring politicians who courageously denounce their past lives and seek to re-establish our nation's moral foundation. More than advice columns or engaging writing, these persons lift hope, strengthen courageous resolve, and authentically lead the way we should go. And we need virtuous politicians, as oxymoronic as that may appear. In fact, the late Bishop Carl Fisher lamented that so few Catholics were involved politically *as true practicing Catholics.*

Serge Abad Gallardo, a former senior official of the French government, is one example of a foreign influence. In *Confessions of a Former Freemason Officer, Converted to Catholicism* (National Catholic Register 2/14/2020), Gallardo describes the diabolical freemasonry that he once embraced as the pathway to a better world. His conversion was sudden, by a strong light at the Shrine of Our Lady of Lourdes in 2012 though it followed a prayerful visit to the statue of St. Therese of Lisieux at Narbonne Cathedral during a family crisis. He noted, and for our better understanding, that a priest shared: "God sometimes lets Satan act so that Satanic temptations and actions can contribute to the man's salvation…with the human's beings will." Since then, fortitude has been a steady grace for this once successful man now shunned by his former allies but grateful to "open some consciences" with his books.

CONVERSION STORY

<u>Msg. Ronald Knox; A Story: The Spirit and Letter of the Law</u>

Born into a staunch Anglican family, in 1888, Ronald Knox was blessed to have two grandfathers who were Anglican bishops. However, although Ronald, himself, was ordained as an Anglican priest in 1912 and appointed chaplain of Trinity College, he left in 1917 when he converted to Roman Catholicism and was ordained a priest in 1918.

For those of us struggling with the challenges of the day that "rub us the wrong way," it might be well to recall that persons like Ronald became pearls of wisdom perhaps from just such tension of their time. World War I, and its effects alone, would lead Monsignor to the doors of the Catholic Church.

Yet, while he wrote many great works and apologetics of the faith, Knox was also noted for his radio personality and detective stories. Considered charitable and well balanced in his writings, he nonetheless believed that his book Enthusiasm was his best. Therein, he analyzed various movements throughout history, Catholic and non-Catholic and concluded that where religious emotion occurred in the absence of doctrine and authority, havoc ensued.

This may be most wonderfully illustrated by the following excerpt from one biography:

> *During World War I, young men facing their own mortality and in need of a rightful conscience, were being drawn to the Catholic faith but sought his counsel. When he intensely reflected on reasons why or why not to enter the Catholic Church, one pivotal incident came to mind. A friend of his had his application refused because in an interview with an Anglican Chaplain-General when he was asked what he would do for a dying man, he answered, "Hear his confession and give him absolution."*

The supposed correct answer was "Give him a cigarette and take any last message he may have for his family." This may be why Msgr. Knox once remarked, "The Anglican Church does not have a leg to stand on."

In today's twisted world, under the auspices of false religion and environmentalism, the dying man would never be given a cigarette and perhaps hastened to death.

Rosary Intentions

As you pray this Sorrowful Mystery, ask that your and everyone's guardian angel reminds them of a daily examination of conscience, regular Confession, and trust in the Holy Spirit to provide wise counsel for self, spouse (or close friend), family, neighbors (including perceived enemies or doubters), clergy and religious, educators, health care workers, business persons (including attorneys), politicians (elected, appointed, government employees), and public figures (including communicators and entertainers).

THE SORROWFUL MYSTERIES (John 1:19-28; 2:1-12; 3:31-36; Mark 9:2-8; John: 6)

First Decade *The Agony in the Garden: My sacrifice Oh God, is a broken spirit; a broken and contrite heart, you, God, will not despise. (Psalm 51:17)* **Or: Seeing the Plank in my eye vs. the Sliver in others?? For: Contrition of Self vs. Condemnation of Others.**

Add a personal faith quote or a prayer intention of your own at the end of this chapter to aid in your meditation:

_____
_____
_____
_____
_____
_____
_____
_____
_____
_____
_____
_____
_____
_____
_____
_____

Helping ourselves and others to **FAITHFULLY** *follow Jesus Christ.*

Section Three - Sorrowful Fortitude
Chapter Two

In 1902, a 20-year-old neighboring farmhand, Alessando Serenelli, attempted to rape 11 year old Goretti. While Serenelli had made sexual advances before, she rejected him each time in the name of God. This time, she rejected him again, shouting, "No! It is a sin! God does not want it!" When Goretti declared that she would rather die, Serenelli stabbed her 14 times.

After being rushed to a hospital, she underwent surgery without anesthesia. She died the following day. Before going to heaven, she forgave her murderer, declaring, "Yes, for the love of Jesus I forgive him….."
Saint Maria Goretti
(1890-1902)

SORROWFUL MYSTERIES

Fortitude

Temperance directs chastity, and seeks to permeate the passions and appetites of the senses with reason. (CCC 2341) However, in many and exceptional cases, this virtue also requires fortitude to resist strong contemporary temptations to violate one's own body along with someone else's. More succinctly stated, some relationships are open to sexual contact, such as in Holy Matrimony, but other life states by choice or orientation forbid such behavior outright. Therefore, same sex behavior is not permitted. For forty-five years Courage RC International (See Resources) has assisted many in carrying this heavy cross and overcoming societal pressure. However, anyone who struggles with chastity outside of Holy Matrimony, including religious and intentionally single persons, should ever implore the Holy Spirit for discernment and strength against these temptations. (CCC 2846, 2848)

Another point in our oppressive, anti-Christian society, chastity also involves a cultural effort for there is "an interdependence between personal betterment and the improvement of society." (CCC 2344; also see Sixth and Ninth Commandments)

The Second Sorrowful Mystery

The Scourging (Mark 15: 6-15)

Virtue: Purity and Bodily Dignity

Snare: Bodily Abuse and Neglect

<u>Subject of Contemporary Reflection in God's Light</u>: ***Fruits of Chastity vs. Rot of Lust***

Every baptized person is called to lead a chaste life, each according to his particular state of life, maintain the integrity of the powers of life and love within, and oppose any behavior that would impair that dignity. (CCC 2338, 2394). The decades long mantra, "My body, my choice," has embedded, beyond contraception and abortion, culturally lethal attitudes and behaviors that also darken the soul, rupture interpersonal relationships and most vitally with God.

<u>Model Saint to Know and Imitate</u>: The story of the young martyr Saint Maria Goretti illustrates the agelessness of sexual sin and violation of a person's human dignity. Her attacker, who was horribly abused and neglected as a child, was steeped into pornography even in the late 19th century. Maria's heroic resistance echoes today, as we learn of several young women attacked and killed by criminal immigrants who may have their own sordid pasts. Regardless, nothing less than a return to respect for the body and God's precious gift of sexuality will turn around the mounting crisis. People were stunned and horrified, repelled and repulsed by Maria's attacker. Today, such incidents receive a short news cycle and no mention of God. We need to change that, and Maria Goretti is one who may assist.

Patti's Stumble Story

Initially, I had anticipated marrying, as a virgin, in a beautiful Catholic Church wedding. I even imagined my husband would be named John, and many children would follow. By my early twenties, any prospect was not just a disappointment, but all men seemed intent on a physical relationship. It simply did not dawn on me to attend a church youth group, especially as my immediate circle of friends had been found in college, and though Catholic or at least Christian, none practiced their faith. In fact, I was the regular Church-goer who was often teased about such devotion.

At the prompting of someone I trusted, I finally met a man in my early twenties I thought would be my future husband. He came from an Irish Catholic background though we never discussed Faith. (It never impressed upon me that this should have been a critical conversation as soon as other temptations entered). Though soft spoken, the man basically "dumped me" after having his way. After the betrayal, I tried to hold onto a modicum of self-respect. I determined not to become promiscuous, but I was sexually assaulted. Either through shame or despair over my foolishness, as I had trusted this acquaintance, my attitude turned numb about matters of relationships and sex. Still, I tried to hold on to that determination to protect my body, mind, and soul. To worsen matters, my initial confession about my first relationship resulted in a priest saying merely, "Those things happen." If anything, I began to think the Church had changed, but I did nothing to learn truth.

Then I met my future husband, but he was divorced. Over a decade would pass before I began to crawl back to Jesus and wholeheartedly pursue that Truth and then find Love. In reflecting on my earlier decisions, I realized that my main error was a basic disconnect from Faith which also entailed a lack of trust, but also simple obedience. I am fully confident that God has forgiven me, but there are consequences for lack of acknowledgment and respecting God's laws.

<u>Mary's Stumble Story</u>

I am a Baby Boomer from 1959. "Some day, my prince will come..." How I loved the Cinderella story: A simple girl went from sweeping chimney soot and cleaning dirty dishes, to attending a fabulous Ball at the castle, wearing glass slippers; swept away by a man whose intentions were true and honest. You are probably asking yourself how my Catholic faith fits into this silly childhood fairytale? Actually ... prudence, temperance and fortitude reflects in the character of Cinderella. Along with her kind obedience to her punitive and envious extended family, she had a pure innocence that kept her chaste. A concept which was lost on me after I met the man I fell in love with in college. I was ill-prepared to deal with moral permissiveness, and over my head with the notion that I understood the consequences of my 'adult' relationship decisions from a faith-based perspective.

I got wrapped up in the extraneous issues of my boyfriend's life way too fast. I side-lined what I needed to do to progress properly through the stages of spiritual maturity-first. When my boyfriend's Jewish side of his family pressured him to lean into his Jewish ethnicity and break up with me, he struggled with that pressure during our five year relationship. Thinking we were going to be married as agreed, resulted in many realizations years later about self-respect and the virtue of fortitude. Firstly, why did I choose him? My attraction to him was superficial and superfluous, not spiritual. He was funny, handsome, fun, and outgoing. My Catholic heart completely rejected the Prince of Peace who I should have been looking to for guidance as a young adult.

About respecting my body, given one fall from grace after another during this relationship, I can say the downhill slide into a life of unholy living is a slippery slope. It does get easier to sin, my friends. Evil relies on our slide into the abyss—slow and steady—Satan is patient. He waits for us to commit one mortal sin after another until we are completely snared, until we despise ourselves more than he despises the remaining iota of practicing Catholicism left in us after we stumble and fall too many times. And my falls from faith were epic.

I traded off my self-respect for nothing. Jesus said, "Do not give dogs what is holy; and do not throw your pearls before swine lest they trample them under foot and turn to attack you." (Matthew 7:6) Why did I not shake the dust off my feet and move on gracefully from this person with my dignity still intact sooner than later? It was due to the fact that my state of unholy living warped my mind into accepting the philosophy of "free-union" through the women's liberation movement as justification to reject the truth of how and when life begins, how love between a man and a woman is sacred, and the spiritual gifts which are given to a blessed marital union.

<u>Virtue Narrative</u>

Naomi (not real name), a young girl of about twelve years of age smiled at the teacher. Her long flowing blond hair and vivid translucent blue eyes imparted a special innocence, but she held tightly to a family secret. At first the teacher simply accepted the teen as a fledging classroom student with understandable awkwardness after being homeschooled most of her childhood. Test anxiety was the worst obstacle, but there was also a lack of social roundedness, the cause of which would not be revealed until later in the year. As spring brought new life, Naomi blossomed. While not Catholic, it became clear that her faith maintained a strong inner core. Then she confided in her teacher.

Her conception had originated in rape, but her mother had chosen to continue the pregnancy. From that she was most loved and cherished, but admitted it was difficult not to have a natural father figure. Still, her step father provided her with much love and attention, and she was confident that she would prosper. Naomi even seemed proud of her mother and so grateful for life. This just demonstrates that God can use any circumstance to restore purity; transform an evil into goodness; and enable the world to embrace life, not for its initial start but as it has unfolded in grace.

A Contemporary Role Model for this Virtue: Jason and Crystalina Evert

Over the past twenty years, Jason and Crystalina Evert have spoken to over a million people on six continents about the virtue of chastity, according to their website (chastity.com) about the *Chastity Project*. Their primary goal is to reach youth, and they have provided retreats or special presentations to many schools. Crystalina, in particular offers hope in a unique way. She, unlike Jason fell for "We thought we loved each other," and sex destroyed the relationship. She notes that it reduced it to a bodily encounter only.

Encouragingly, students and their parents alike love these events, perhaps because this beautiful couple relate so well with them. Aside from their physical appearances their organization provides answers to questions about dating, and marriage and family. Furthermore, they do not shy from the more controversial areas like LGTBQ, birth control and STDs, as well as "starting over." For those who cannot attend a seminar or special appearance, *Chastity Project* provides numerous helpful books, booklets, CDs, DVDs and apps. They even have a curriculum on life, love, and the theology of the body with a leader's guide, parent's guide, and student work book. Middle school is addressed in a separate set. Jason runs a podcast with a tagline: "Lust is boring" for those who seek special feedback from knowledgeable guests on answering tough questions on dating, singleness, marriage, and sexuality.

CONVERSION STORY

<u>Alessandro Serentelli—Maria Goretti; A Story: A Conversion to Purity by the Courage of a Pure Soul</u>

Alessandro Serentelli's name is quite overshadowed by St. Maria Goretti whom he murdered in 1902. Incredibly this eleven year old child emphatically refused to yield sexually to the overpowering Alessandro, not due to any feminist logic but for the fact that "It is a sin. God does not want it." Alessandro, who had been consumed by pornography and lustful fantasies about Maria, then flew into a rage and stabbed her fourteen times. Yet, even as she lingered in torturous pain before dying, Maria forgave Alessandro. Her purity, courage, and sacrifice would become the most marvelous conversion stories of all time.

Her assailant was sentenced to thirty years of hard labor and for years harbored deep anger and then despair. Maria appeared to him in his cell, smiled in the midst of Lillies, the flower symbol of purity, and from that moment brought Alessandro peace of mind and soul. He later recounted in his Mary 5th, 1961 testimony: "Looking back at my past, I can see that in my early youth, I chose a bad path which led me to ruin myself. My behavior was influenced by print, mass media and bad examples which are followed by the majority of young people even without thinking. I did the same. I was not worried."

Alessandro continued by crediting the intercessory prayers of St. Maria Goretti for saving him and expressed gratitude to the Brothers of St. Francis, Capuchins from Marche who welcomed his as a brother after his release from prison.

In the final paragraph of his spiritual legacy, he wrote: "I hope this letter that I wrote can teach others the happy lesson of avoiding evil and of always following the right path, like little children. I feel that religion with its precepts is not something we can live without, but rather it is a real comfort, the real strength of life and the only safe way in every circumstance, even the most painful ones in life."

Alessandro Serentelli died on May 5th, 1970, in the hopes of witnessing the vision of God and being reunited with his loved ones and his Guardian Angel, Marie.

Rosary Intentions

Note: This particular Mystery calls for sacrificial prayer as so many are confused or misled about the necessity of purity and rightful exercise of the body. Pray for cultural conversion while contemplating Christ's sacrificial perseverance during his Passion and Crucifixion scourging despite excruciating physical and emotional pain. Pray personally for self, spouse, family, neighbor (perceived enemies or doubters), clergy and religious, educators, health care workers, business persons (including attorneys, politicians (elected, appointed, government workers), and public figures (including communicators and entertainers).

THE SORROWFUL MYSTERIES (John 1:19-28; 2:1-12; 3:31-36; Mark 9:2-8; John: 6)

Second Decade *The Scourging: For this is the will of God, your sanctification: that you abstain from sexual immorality. (1 Thessalonians 4:3)* **For: Fruits of Chastity vs. Rot of Lust.**

Add a personal faith quote or a prayer intention of your own at the end of this chapter to aid in your meditation:

*Helping ourselves and others to **FAITHFULLY** follow Jesus Christ.*

Section Three - Sorrowful Fortitude
Chapter Three

"Because Jesus alone is our strength and power in all our weaknesses."
Saint
Anna Schäffer
(1882-1925)

SORROWFUL MYSTERIES

Fortitude

Meekness is often confused with cowardliness, but it is actually a moral virtue that requires great fortitude, for from these "poor"— those humble and meek— the Spirit is making ready "a people prepared for the Lord." (CCC 716). It is the Holy Spirit that makes us discern between trials, which are necessary for the growth of the inner man, and temptation which leads to sin and death. (CCC 2847). Yes, meekness is a trial particularly when the ignorant and debased torments us unjustly, as they did Jesus Christ, mocking his kingship with a crown of thorns. Blessed are the meek, for they will inherit the earth. (CCC 1716).

The Third Sorrowful Mystery

The Crowning of Thorns (Mark 15: 16-20)

Virtue: Courageous Meekness

Snare: Tepidity or Rage

<u>Subject of Contemporary Reflection in God's Light</u>: **Meekness vs. Cowardliness**

Rightful order of authority, natural law, and Divine Will necessitates a proper disposition towards our neighbors even when they behave unjustly toward us. In our volatile society, there is a tendency to either remain quietly anonymous or rage against an unfairness. The former may be a type of 'cowardliness' and the latter a misinterpretation of church beliefs. Heroic meekness may include powerful truth but still expressed in gentle spirit that moves minds and hearts.

<u>Model Saint to Know and Imitate</u>: St. Francis de Sales was often targeted by arrogant Protestant enemies, who also sought his life, but also some within the Catholic Church. He exhibited a high degree of meekness and still brought thousands of souls back to the fullness of Faith. They say he died with stones in his bile likely due to holding his temper on many occasions to project a gentle spirit. He denounced rash judgement and insisted that persons must use extreme caution when speaking of another person's actions or person.

<u>Patti's Stumbling Story</u>

Dr. Bernard Nathanson, the once infamous abortionist who converted and later championed life stood before the conference crowd and ably explained the horrors of abortion. As one who had neglected and even abused the dignity of my body, I was amazed to discover I did not even know my body. Oh, the understanding of "sperm meets egg" and that was how babies were conceived was clear. I had even scoffed at those ignorant women who thought they could become pregnant from various myths, like sitting on a toilet with sperm.. How proud— focus on that word—I was that I chose the contraceptive pill in a phase of "sexual responsibility" while others "carelessly" or indifferently engaged in sex without such protection.

I was an idiot. I did not even know for decades how the pill worked thinking it prevented the fertile cycle entirely. It would be years before I learned that I may have actually aborted fertilized eggs and guilty of the same sin I was condemning. Yet, it was even worse than that. The pill, I have no doubt, so messed up by reproductive system, I nearly died in childbirth from hemorrhaging. The doctor could never explain the need for an emergency hysterectomy at that juncture but I had already decided not to have more children. (Note the "I" there.). God let me know that he could quite arrange that Himself. In later years, I read an article that linked the contraceptive pill to the weakening of the uterus.

Back to the late Dr. Nathanson for another lesson learned: Over thirty years ago, he chillingly foretold a Frankenstein type scenario. By 20 weeks a female fetus's ovaries have a lifetime supply of 6-7 million eggs (babycenter.com). If such females were / are aborted, modern science could potentially "harvest" those eggs for such procedures as IVF . That would mean a person could be born from a mother who never lived outside the womb—who was never born. How foolishly I had made decisions about my body, intake of substances, reckless behavior. How absolutely tragic that a female fetus would be killed but her eggs used for later merchandizing and profit. However, thank you Sweet Jesus, that I was not a child of such a victim.

<u>Mary's Stumbling Story</u>

I am guilty for many decades of voting for political leaders who have displayed characteristics of cowardliness by glad-handing and smooth-talking voters just to get elected and then, once comfortable in the safety of their limitless terms, they ultimately make their grab for power. Yet, I forced myself to look past the moral character of many politicians and swallow the bitter pill for the political party. Gulp! I might not have voted so uncritically if I had applied Jesus's teachings from the Sermon on the Mount.

As a voter, I have contributed to this unhealthy political environment which we find ourselves living in today. Meek and gentle politicians are rare gems. In fact, the concept of a meek politician is possibly an oxymoron. Meekness doesn't get votes.

As I misstep over how to vote with a good conscience, I wonder how can I not vote and still fulfill my civic duty as an American? What are my faith-based political choices going forward? Jesus avoided the politics of men. Jesus knew politics was complicated even then. He subtly told the people to make the best choices regarding Caesar or God. He offered: Give to each—wisely. It is hard to serve two masters.

In prayer, I feel I must choose first to follow the God of the Bible and not the gods of politics. Jesus never mixed the two. What's the lesson He was trying to teach in his conversation with Pontius Pilate before His crucifixion? Basically: Politics is a necessary contentious 'evil' and belongs to men in this world and Jesus is from a loving and peaceful world where politics and political gamesmanship has no place and no position in God's Kingdom.

As a voter, politics has lead me into uncharitable thoughts, judgmental behavior, and into making inferior candidate voting choices. Going forward, I must be careful to not sacrifice the integrity of my soul just so that I can put a "I Voted" sticker on my chest for the world to see. Will God judge me poorly if my party candidate is a morally compromised person or I choose NOT to vote at all? Or, will I be judged by God if I DO vote for a person who acts against God's commandments and teachings just to say I voted?

Virtue Narrative

The woman attendee froze, stunned into silence. Father Paul Marx was circulating among attendees at the Human Life International Conference (HLI) in the early 90's, thanking everyone for their pro life work. As the now late world traveler and social scientist priest moved, a gentle smile remained fixed on a jovial face.

Here was the paragon of service, matched only by the likes of history's most charitable, wandering Saints. Father Marx, most self deflecting and even meek, had visited multitudes of countries and villages over the decades to report on nefarious government programs of sterilization and other foreign propaganda attacking their cultures and families, and to respond to the people's needs. He was often a lone figure who sustained the dignity of all the world's forgotten persons, but most of all to bring them Jesus Christ.

Moreover, Father Marx produced excellent newsletters covering many countries around the globe, perfect supplements to any social studies class. His descriptions of the geography and various cultural tidbits and statistics were only outmatched by his disclosure of the evil that was occurring in these regions by global interests in contracting and mutilating the native people.

Still, most powerful about Father Marx was his incredible ability to seek the truth in love. He never shied away from the conversation of abortion, even for youth, but managed to ensure the authority of parents and individuals to respond to that truth.

A Contemporary Role Model for this Virtue: Jennifer Hubbard

Jennifer Hubbard, frequent contributor to *Magnificat Magazine* and author of *Finding Sanctuary* (Ave Maria Press, 2021), lost her six-year-old daughter, Catherine, during the Sandy Hook Elementary School shooting in Newton, Connecticut on December 14, 2012.

Jennifer asserts she felt a quietness and serenity in her immediate grief. Yet, she deeply suffered further when her father died, and her marriage ended. However, she had to survive for her son, two years older than Catherine. There she found purpose and grace. Also, a chance error in Catherine's obituary led Jennifer to start the Catherine Violet Hubbard Animal Sanctuary. Journaling also provided the grieving mother with an outlet for that which would later give her deeper understanding of her heart and reflections about faith.

Ironically, Jennifer recalls that she had actually been growing her in faith shortly before tragedy struck, and she wrestled with the typical reaction of questioning why God would let this happen to her. Ultimately, she reconciled her anger and grumbling with acceptance of God's will, and that someday He would make all things understood and right in His perfect plan.

(*Authors Note: Rage-filled fury often spills from those who have lost a loved one to violence. Politicians and advocates may follow suit, yet overcoming those impulses marks a true child of God. Furthermore we cannot equate meekness with powerlessness.*)

CONVERSION STORY

<u>A Story: The Tales of Royalty Who Sought the Crown of the Everlasting Kingdom</u>

Who does not enjoy an engaging story involving faithful royalty or their close advisors and colleagues, who embraced the Roman Catholic Church and valued the crown of heaven more than the earthly lineage and wealth? History is replete with such examples of persons who exchanged their jeweled crowns for a crown of thorns.

Among these are a granddaughter of Queen Victoria, Victoria Eugenie of Battenberg who converted from the Church of England to Roman Catholicism to marry King Alfonso of Spain. Despite the gross infidelity of her husband, she devoted herself to helping the sick and poor, including the Spanish Red Cross. Pope Pius XI would confer on her the Golden Rose in the Church's appreciation.

After hearing Pope John Paul II on EWTN, Lord Nicholas Windsor became the first royal male to convert in four centuries, in 2001. This also required giving up his right to succession to the British throne, as he sought a different throne, in a different kingdom. The same is true of Princess Alexandra of Hanover, descendent of Queen Victoria and granddaughter of Grace Kelly.

Katharine, Duchess of Kent, received the Queen's approval when she converted in 1994 for reasons of personal faith. Considering she was married to the late Queen Elizabeth's cousin, this took true conviction, a leap of faith and courage.

Most recently, in 2019, Queen Elizabeth granted her Anglican Chaplain, Gavin Ashenden, permission to convert to Catholicism.

Initially, Princess Charlene of Monaco was included as a contemporary convert in 2010. Sadly, some controversy swirls about her today. However, her challenges remind us that all of our faith journeys can be bumpy or derailed, emphasizing that need for constant prayer.

(As a side note, *Magnificat Magazine's library has many more of these signs of hope.*)

Rosary Intentions

Pray for the renewal of the world and conversion of souls through gentle meekness but courageous acts of truth and love, by self, spouse or close friends, family, neighbors including perceived enemies or doubters), clergy and religious, educators, health care workers, business persons (including attorneys), politicians (elected, appointed, government employees), and public figures (including communicators and entertainers).

THE SORROWFUL MYSTERIES (John 1:19-28; 2:1-12; 3:31-36; Mark 9:2-8; John: 6)

Third Decade: *The Crowning of Thorns: Blessed are the meek, for they will inherit the earth (Beatitude, Matt 5:5)* **For: Meekness vs. Cowardliness.**

Add a personal faith quote or a prayer intention of your own at the end of this chapter to aid in your meditation:

_____
_____
_____
_____
_____
_____
_____
_____
_____
_____
_____
_____
_____
_____
_____
_____
_____
_____

Helping ourselves and others to **FAITHFULLY** *follow Jesus Christ.*

Section Three - Sorrowful Fortitude
Chapter Four

"Let us not forget that Jesus not only suffered, but also rose in glory; so, too, we go to the glory of the Resurrection by way of suffering and the Cross."

Saint Maximilian Kolbe
(1894-1941)

Saint Maximilian Kolbe was a Polish Franciscan friar. 83 years ago, he died as a Catholic martyr in Auschwitz.

SORROWFUL MYSTERIES

Fortitude

Perhaps one could be meek for a short period of time or in particular insulting incidents, but to courageously persevere in that state as Jesus Christ achieved throughout His life, but most intensely in His Passion would try our tolerance. In fact without his example—His constancy in doing the good (CCC 1808), would any mortal even the most holy of the martyrs have ever achieved that status without Jesus's startling but sterling example? "The children of our holy mother Church rightly hope for the grace of final perseverance and the recompense of God their Father for the good works accomplished with his grace in communion with Jesus." (CCC 2016)

The Fourth Sorrowful Mystery

The Carrying of the Cross (Luke 23: 26-32)

Virtue: Perseverance

Snare: Mocking or Rejecting the Cross

<u>Subject of Contemporary Reflection in God's Light</u>: ***Perseverance vs. Resentment***

The false and empty pursuit of Utopia in the temporal world leads to the demise of one's salvation. "The order and harmony of the created world results from the diversity of beings and from the relationships that exist among them. The beauty of creation reflects the infinite beauty of the Creator and ought to inspire the respect and submission of man's intellect and will." (CCC 341) Nothing is lastingly gained without the cross, and everyone has a cross to bear, regardless of power, wealth, or other circumstances. There will be periods of dryness; our wills wounded by pride. (CCC 2728) We must pray that we walk the talk…especially the final walk at death.

<u>Model Saint to Know and Imitate</u>: Maximillian Kolbe the Concentration Camp Martyr, not only picked up a fellow prisoner's cross—condemnation of death—but lifted it from the pleading man's shoulders in order to provide him a chance of reunion with his family after World War II. That sacrifice would entail being starved to death in a hot box, but failing that being poisoned. The man he saved, Franciszek Gajowniczek, a Roman Catholic, would spend his life—so long as he had breath in his lungs—telling people about this heroic act.

Patti's Stumble Story

Whenever I am tempted to pounce on all the agnostics and atheists of the world, and closer to "home," fellow dissident Catholics, I must remind myself—although sometimes it is Jesus who does the head knocking—that I was once a fallen away Catholic who thought she had great answers to anyone who challenged my waywardness and political opinions. I recall one such smug moment in time.

Following the birth of my first son, we rationalized that we could not afford another child. The economy had recessed and work was difficult to find for both of us. Certainly God understood that the smart course would be … contraception. I would never abort, so was not that the better "choice"? I confidently entered the local county offices for the pills although I had to complete an orientation first. As I sat amid numerous younger girls, many high school age, I recall my critical observations. Chatting amongst themselves and ignoring what the counselor was relaying about the proper and effective uses of contraception, I had the scornful thought that they would likely end up pregnant either through careless use of the contraception or not using the means properly. Again, I had every intention to follow through effectively.

I did not know, as mentioned previously in my willful arrogance, that chemical contraception could actually cause the abortion of the littlest embryo, flushed from the lining of the theoretically life giving uterine wall.

I just thought I was being conscientious. I had no conscience, so that was a lie in itself.

Eventually, I ceased the pill for other concerns, and I did become pregnant again.

Had I learned my lesson? Not really. Though I would not abort, this time I would ensure that there was no chance of further pregnancies.

However, I digress. Here I had mocked young girls who were in actuality "tossing their crosses," as I, the elder, was also doing likewise. What if instead, I had counseled them, even if they had rejected me? I will never know, but I can pray for their souls, even now. Someday, I pray to meet each in Heaven where we can show our mutual forgiveness and love.

Mary's Stumble Story

If I am faced with the temptation to speak about others, or to engage in gossip about an individual, it is always when I am in the company of others and "group-think" has emboldened us to make comments about a person we do not know and have never met personally. This kind of modern action or reaction is akin to the behavior in the Bible of picking up a stone and casting it at another person with total disregard for the plank in my eye or the sins on my soul. (John 8:7)

This is really difficult to admit, (I brought this matter into confession on more than one occasion) but I engaged in snickering and a gossipy mentality with my girlfriends even when I was in Catholic elementary school. The Us versus Them mentality would often kick in during lunchtime when our group would sit and watch other kids move around the school yard. What fun we had picking on others and giggling with one another while casually eating our lunch. We would chat among ourselves about somebody's new haircut, or how poorly they played dodge ball that day, or the sloppiness or height of their school uniform skirt, or their bucked teeth, etc. I never stopped to ask myself, then, if I would have had the courage to act like that if I was sitting next to Jesus on the school yard bench! I think we all know the answer to that question. So why can human beings be so judgmental and cruel in the perceived absence of God's presence? Free will? Peer pressure? Gang mentality?

Near the Mount of Olives, when Jesus confronted those who were casting stones in an effort to kill a woman for committing adultery, Jesus asked the crowd if any were there without sin and would like to participate in killing her. Mumbling and stumbling... no one took the stone from His hand. Of course not! Why can we not all be like Jesus and have the fortitude to ask the same question of our friends or family when we feel emboldened or pressured to participate in modern verbal stoning? It just takes one courageous person to say: "And who are you to judge?" That question might lose us some 'friends'— yes?

Ironically, as time went on, I came to understand that those individuals whom I had once made fun of with my friends at school were really good people who were carrying their own crosses like I was. I became life-long friends with two of them! In hindsight, Jesus was sitting next to me on that schoolyard bench while we were gossiping about other kids. I was so busy making remarks I didn't take the spiritual time to listen to Him.

Virtue Narrative

Stories abound of women who have sacrificed money, position, and even all they possess to follow the will of God, some carrying incredibly heavy crosses. A few, like abortion survivors, live their lives with suffering but enormous gratitude for their lives. One such persons carried her cross lying down, confined to a gurney all her life. Sadly, there was no clip found upon researching this show.

She was a guest on the Sally Jessy Rafael show. Sally was a TV hostess back in the 1980s (through 2012) who touted all the platitudes of modern feminism and was obstinately pro abortion. The young woman guest lay flat while interviewed but not "heard" and seemed oblivious to her cheerful disposition. As Sally blabbed all about the horrors of inaccessibility to "safe" abortions, it seemed painfully obvious that the young woman was intended to impress upon the audience the outcome of a botched abortion. In other words, without legal abortion, look what has happened to one person, a woman, now entrapped for her life, never to be free to do what she wanted.

Here was the surprise which Sally actually seemed not to hear. The woman on the gurney rejoiced in her life; she spoke of being grateful that she had survived.. Stunningly, Sally simply talked right over that declaration.

Imagine if someone asked the woman if she felt like she was carrying a cross, she might have agreed to some extent. However, for her, the gurney was not a cross but something that uplifted and moved her while she could still experience other aspects of living.

Where is this woman today? Is she alive? We do not know, but certainly if she has passed away, she is running free in the Kingdom of God.

Where is Sally? Where are the Sallies of the world now or heading? They need our prayers and extra sacrifices.

A Contemporary Role Model for this Virtue: Ed Jozsa

While not attesting to its veracity, the reconversion story of one man brought back to the life, and back to Jesus Christ after a near fatal car accident, emphasizes the many graces of carrying a cross. Ed Jozsa, a successful airline pilot, should have died in the horrific crash, and doctors were baffled at how he survived. However, Ed, also author of *The Mystic Next Door*, and popular public speaker, claims to have seen his life as one that would have been damned, speaks of the excruciating misery of the absence of God which he experienced for a time, and the horror of the dark abyss for those not living in accord with God. Though he deemed himself a "good"

Catholic, what he saw and experienced informed him that he was not. Today, he extols people to carry their crosses and once remarked that if he had to endure one hundred years of horrible pain, that would be worth it for reunion with the glory of God which he also claims he experienced.

CONVERSION STORY

<u>A Story: Seeking Suffering in Reparation for the Rending of the Church</u>

Anna Ivanovna Abrikosova (1882-1936) was born into privilege and an ample supply of chocolate as her family was the official supplier of confections to the Russian Imperial Court, but her parents died, relatively early in her life. After she traveled following marriage, she was afforded the opportunity to study a number of Catholic books. St. Catherine of Siena profoundly impressed her, and she converted to Catholicism in 1908. However, due to canonical law, she would be considered Greek Catholic.

After further searching, Anna rested in the Dominican spirituality and eventually moved her husband to become Catholic, as well. Yet, in an ironic twist, when they formally requested the Pope to become Roman Catholic, they were refused. This would lead them back to Russia and eventual persecution for their faith. During those years, though, Anna's husband would become a priest, and she, in turn, would take monastic vows as a Dominican sister, found a Dominican Third Order, and become Mother Catherine.

Arrested for her faith, Mother Catherine was imprisoned from 1924-1932 when a friend petitioned Stalin himself for her release.

However, she had been diagnosed with breast cancer, and between that and renewing her affiliation with the Dominican order, which resulted in her rearrest in 1933, Anna died at the age of 54 in the Butyrka Prison Infirmary in 1936.

Considered a martyr for the faith, Anna (Mother Catherine) was known for two ringing quotes that indicate her joy in carrying her cross: "I wish to lead a uniquely supernatural life and to accomplish *to the end* of my vow of immolation for the priest and for Russia." Also, "Which of you, in a moment of fervor, has not asked Christ for the grace of participating in his sufferings?"

<u>Rosary Intentions</u>

Pray for the grace to patiently persevere and endure to carry whatever cross God sends for ourselves, spouses or close friends, family, neighbor (including perceived enemies or doubters), clergy and religious, educators, heath care workers, business persons (including attorneys), politicians (elected, appointed, government employees), public figurers (including communicators and entertainers).

THE SORROWFUL MYSTERIES (John 1:19-28; 2:1-12; 3:31-36; Mark 9:2-8; John: 6)

Fourth Decade: *The Carrying of the Cross:* He who perseveres unto the end will be saved. *(Mathew 10:22)* **For: Perseverance vs Resentful Resistance.**

Add a personal faith quote or a prayer intention of your own at the end of this chapter to aid in your meditation:

_____
_____
_____
_____
_____
_____
_____
_____
_____
_____
_____
_____
_____
_____
_____
_____
_____
_____
_____

*Helping ourselves and others to **FAITHFULLY** follow Jesus Christ.*

Section Three - Sorrowful Fortitude
Chapter Five

"And when night comes, and you look back over the day and see how fragmentary everything has been, and how much you planned that has gone undone, and all the reasons you have to be embarrassed and ashamed: just take everything exactly as it is, put it in God's hands and leave it with Him."

Saint Theresa Benedicta of the Cross aka Edith Stein
Baptized Catholic in 1922.
Murdered in the gas chamber at Birkenau in 1942.

SORROWFUL MYSTERIES

Fortitude

"Greater love has no one than this, than to lay down one's life for one's friends." (John 15:13). Jesus also died for his enemies, and elsewhere admonishes us to do good to our enemies. This is extraordinary courage, as we naturally flee death, but we might risk our lives for those we love. To do so for strangers or those who revile us, mandates a pure heart. "Martyrdom is the supreme witness given to the truth of the faith; it means bearing witness even unto death. He endures death through an act of fortitude." (CCC 2473). "Moreover, many martyrs died for not adoring "the Beast," refusing to even simulate such worship." (CCC 2113).

The Fifth Sorrowful Mystery

The Crucifixion (John 19: 17-30)

Virtue: Sacrifice and Surrender

Snare: Mocking Jesus Christ, Idolatry

<u>Subject of Contemporary Reflection in God's Light</u>: **Surrender to God vs. Resignation to Evil**

Even white martyrdom entails death by a thousand cuts. Daily we must be faithful despite the loss of family, friends, prestige, reputation, and even employment. Some will face imprisonment. Yet, the sign of perfect martyrdom is to submit to such humiliation for the salvation of souls.

(Special Note: See *Cambrai Homily* which is the earliest known Irish homily, dating to the 7th or early 8th century, which is housed in the Médiathèque d'agglomération de Cambrai and discusses the three colors of martyrdom: white, red, blue (or green).)

<u>Model Saint to Know and Imitate</u>: St. Peter learned the hard way, and one could speculate that he denied Jesus Christ not just for fear of death, but that given the arrest of Jesus Christ, anyone who followed him would likewise be intensely mocked and degraded and killed. (Matthew 16:24)

<u>Patti's Stumble Story</u>

"How dare they" was one of my repetitive mental if not vocal refrains in the '80s. I just knew I was in the right about so many situations negatively affecting my life. One incident occurred when returning home from a hard day's work, I turned on the hall switch without any results. I tripped in the dark and fell. The electric company had turned off the power. Now, I do not recall if we had just paid it, or they failed to give us a notice, but I was nonetheless infuriated at "the injustice and injury." I was going to sue. I called the utility company

which did turn on power, and then an attorney. He consulted with me briefly; I did not have a case. How dare he!

In retrospect, even if the power company had been a bit more accommodating, I have to admit that our discipline with money, when we had any, was imprudent. In retrospect, we worked hard, but I would have likely given our citizenship a "C" at best in such matters, and we utterly failed in any citizenship of Heaven. In short, it amazes me even today that I was so blind to excesses of expressive emotionalism that lacked wisdom. It seemed we lived in the dark literally and figuratively.

Yet, at no time in that stretch of my life did I offer anything to God, monetarily, physically, emotionally, or spiritually. So, all those temporal sufferings netted me nada in my heavenly "savings account."

I also had to acknowledge that if I could have been that selfish and negatively relational with some people around me then, how could I not understand similar souls in this age?

That this new generation had even less faith taught and lived around them than I had only highlights that it was previous generations that started the ball rolling downhill. So, it makes sense that so many not only scoff at carrying a cross—suffering in anyway—but they double down on blaming others, all the while being incognizant of God in their midst.

Mary's Stumble Story

In 1985, I took a trip to Italy with my parents. My mother and father were well acquainted with Father Joseph Pius Martin through a woman named Vera Calandra. Father Martin was the priest who *had been a caretaker and friend to Padre Pio in San Giovanni Rotondo in the last three years of Padre Pio's life. During a conversation with Father Martin one evening, I asked him about Padre Pio and the stigmata. I look back on this conversation I had with Father Martin at the dinner table in San Giovanni and feel so ashamed for my lack of faith! I asked him, "Father Martin, is it true? Did Padre Pio really have the stigmata? Did his hands and feet really bleed....did you actually see it?"*

My parents sat at the table, oddly silent and stiff, and like me awaited Father Martin's hopefully patient reply to my graceless question. ('Oh ye of little faith' I was.... to even suggest this was some kind of ploy that had been perpetrated on the faithful!) Father Martin looked at me with brotherly patience, took a breath, and with solemnity said, "Yes, Mary, I saw Padre Pio's wounds. I personally tended to the stigmata wounds and helped clean them. I also tended to the bruises and wounds he endured from the Devil who would enter his room at night." Father Martin's face looked so weighted down…..his sadness was palpable for the cross Padre Pio was given to carry. I was speechless—shocked—I had no words.

At the end of our dinner, Father Martin looked at me and my parents and told us he wanted us to go to the Vatican the next day. He said "something special" was going to happen there and he wanted us to be a part of it. What that "special" thing was we did not know. Father Martin gave us instructions on where to go, what steps to climb, who to talk to and that we would be directed to an inner courtyard inside the Vatican to receive a "special blessing."

The next day as we stood in an inner courtyard inside the Vatican with about thirty nuns and the invited group of lay people, I noticed a small nun with a bit of a hunch who came blustering past me to talk to a priest standing about eight feet from where we stood. It was Mother Teresa! She wanted to see the Pope—she had to talk with him she told this priest. Suddenly, within a few minutes, a window up above us in this private courtyard opened and there appeared Pope John Paul II. As close as I can ever be, I could see his face as he smiled so sweetly at us and waved. We all looked up at him, all of us taking one another's hands immediately in stunned reverence, as the Pope greeted us and gave us a private blessing. Mother Teresa looked up at him and received his blessing, as well. Afterward, Pope John Paul II waved at us one more time and closed his window as Mother Theresa quickly exited the courtyard and went up some stairs.

Father Joseph Martin had sent us to the Vatican for a special, private blessing from Pope John Paul II and to see Mother Teresa in person! My intellect never again stumbled or questioned the validity of the stigmata or the immense suffering saints like Padre Pio endure.

Virtue Narrative

Ruth Minsky Sender is a survivor of the Holocaust, and in three riveting memoirs, she shares her account of great suffering for many decades. They include *The Cage*, *To Life*, and *The Holocaust Lady*. An exceptional survivor, this eventual teacher shared the hardship and cruelties she endured but never with bitterness. What most appeals is what is threaded throughout her writing which includes poetry, is the message of hope…with an emphasis on the celebration of life. She writes: "Surviving one more day in the camps was spiritual resistance." Or, perhaps, it was also a bit of spiritual warfare on her part, too.

Ruth often wrote of the value of life and lives in love for those all around her. For many years she shared her story, visited schools, and participated in events, and though candid about the horror of the Holocaust, the former Polish native's purpose was to inspire. Even when one of her sons died of cancer in 2018 and she suffered two bouts of cancer, Ruth, originally Riva, exuberantly went optimistically forward.

As a Jew, Ruth may not have understood Jesus willingly being crucified. Still, there is no doubt that Ruth did not resent her own cross even while detesting it, but saw through her suffering the incredible gift of life. She never surrendered that or her spirit. As of this writing, eternal life. Ruth is approaching 100 years old, but one can imagine her finally commending her own spirit to eternal life.

A Contemporary Role Model for this Virtue: Alveda King

One can be in awe that the future pro life civil rights leader, Alveda King, niece of Martin Luther King, Jr. was born on January 22 (1951), the same date, twenty two years later that would mark the Roe vs. Wade Supreme Court ruling that changed the course of law regarding abortion and American history. Born in Atlanta, the eldest of five children, she recalled the racist violence that threatened her family home, as her father was also a well known civil rights activist. This former member of the Georgia House of Representatives, Alveda would one day courageously and sacrificially set a path at odds from most of her family, one that would result in a serious separation over the rights of the unborn.

However, in the beginning, Alveda appeared to be on track living the dream of a post Civil Rights era Black woman. Sociology and journalism were two areas of interest. But pregnancy would appear as a barrier. Finding herself pregnant on two occasions, abortion seemed the only resolution. She once declared that she "drank the Kool-Aid" because she thought it was the answer.

In one moving quote, after repenting in 1982, the fiery advocate said: "I prayed often for the deliverance from the pain caused by my decision to abort my baby. And truly for me and countless abortive mothers, nothing on earth can fully restore what has been lost; only Jesus can." In the Silent Nor More Awareness Campaign, her testimony of two abortions speaks to God's forgiveness and healing.

It was not until the birth of her first child that Alveda saw through what she later remarked were lies. Yet, the upheaval in the aftermath of these choices would seriously hamper her private live, as she was married and divorced three times. Still, she insists that marriage is the bedrock of solid family life.

Regardless, she did not look back but reared her six children and became consistently protective of life from womb to the tomb. Along the way, she still received a Master's in Business Management and later an honorary degree from Saint Anselm College in New Hampshire. At the same time, she was becoming more vocal about the abhorrence of abortion.

In one post after another and across the nation, this prominent conservative leader, evangelist, and author has fearlessly and faithfully challenged the status quo of "pro choice" everywhere and in a pronounced way within the African American community. Boldly she insisted that the (King's) Dream could not be kept alive if we murder the children. She also claimed that abortion and racism stem from the same poisonous root, selfishness.

Among the achievements of this notable leader are the Alveda King Ministries and other organizations with the purposes of education in faith and life issues, such as Speak for Life. Though health issues have somewhat hampered her mobility, this seemingly tireless defender of the most defenseless works on several boards, including Priests for Life. In 2011, this blessed grandmother was given the Cardinal John O'Conner Pro-Life Hall of Fame Award, and in 2021, she received the Presidential Lifetime Achievement Award.

CONVERSION STORY

Edith Stein, St. Theresa Benedicta of the Cross; A Story: A Convert Surrenders Her Heart and Fortifies the Heart of Her Church

The 20th Century witnessed the greatest bloodshed of all human history in various global wars and as a consequence of the great evils of fascism and communism. Incredibly, though, numerous individual souls made reparation for the tyrants who slaughtered millions of innocent people. Among these giants was St. Edith Stein.

Although the modern world would prefer to think that holy people are cognitively disabled sheep, Edith's keen intellect was observed from an early age. Born to a Jewish family, Edith enjoyed academic success throughout her early life and later attended the University of Breslau, Gottingen University and the University of Freiburg as a graduate assistant.

During her teen years, a crisis of faith resulted in disbelief though she continued attending services. After encountering the Roman Catholic faith during college and exploring the New Testament, she would become convinced of the truth of Christianity and converted to Catholicism in 1921.

Nonetheless, when Hitler came to power, her Jewish lineage would lead to her expulsion as a university lecturer. So, she turned her attention to writing in order to bridge Judaism and Christianity and explored St. Thomas Aquinas, among other "searches for the truth" despite the fact that much of her works would not be published until after her death.

Knowing that her life was endangered, as early as 1938, Edith fled to the Netherlands where she was joined by her sister, Rosa, also a convert to the faith. However, when the Nazi's invaded that region, and her sister was not permitted a Swiss passport, Edith determined to stay with her loved one. Eventually both siblings would be sent to Auschwitz where they would meet the same fate as so many other Jews.

In the ensuing years, Edith's work would come to the favorable attention of Catholic leaders, and she was beatified and then canonized, albeit amid some controversy from the Jewish community. Nevertheless, she is considered a martyr for the faith and held in high esteem as St. Teresa Benedicta of the Cross.

Rosary Intentions

May Our Lord Jesus Christ's loving gaze from the Cross move me, spouse or close friend, family, neighbor (including enemies or doubters), clergy and religious, educators, health care workers, business persons (including attorneys), politicians (elected, appointed, government employees), public figures (including communicators and entertainers) *to know Agape, Love in Perfection, bear suffering with receptive love and pray for conversion (CCC 1435).*

THE SORROWFUL MYSTERIES (John 1:19-28; 2:1-12; 3:31-36; Mark 9:2-8; John: 6)

Fifth Decade: *The Crucifixion: Trust in the Lord with all your heart and lean not on your own understanding; in all your ways submit to him, and he will make our paths straight. (Proverbs 3:5-6)* **For: Surrender to God vs Resignation to Evil.**

Add a personal faith quote or a prayer intention of your own at the end of this chapter to aid in your meditation:

_____
_____
_____
_____
_____
_____
_____
_____
_____
_____
_____
_____
_____
_____
_____
_____
_____
_____

*Helping ourselves and others to **FAITHFULLY** follow Jesus Christ.*

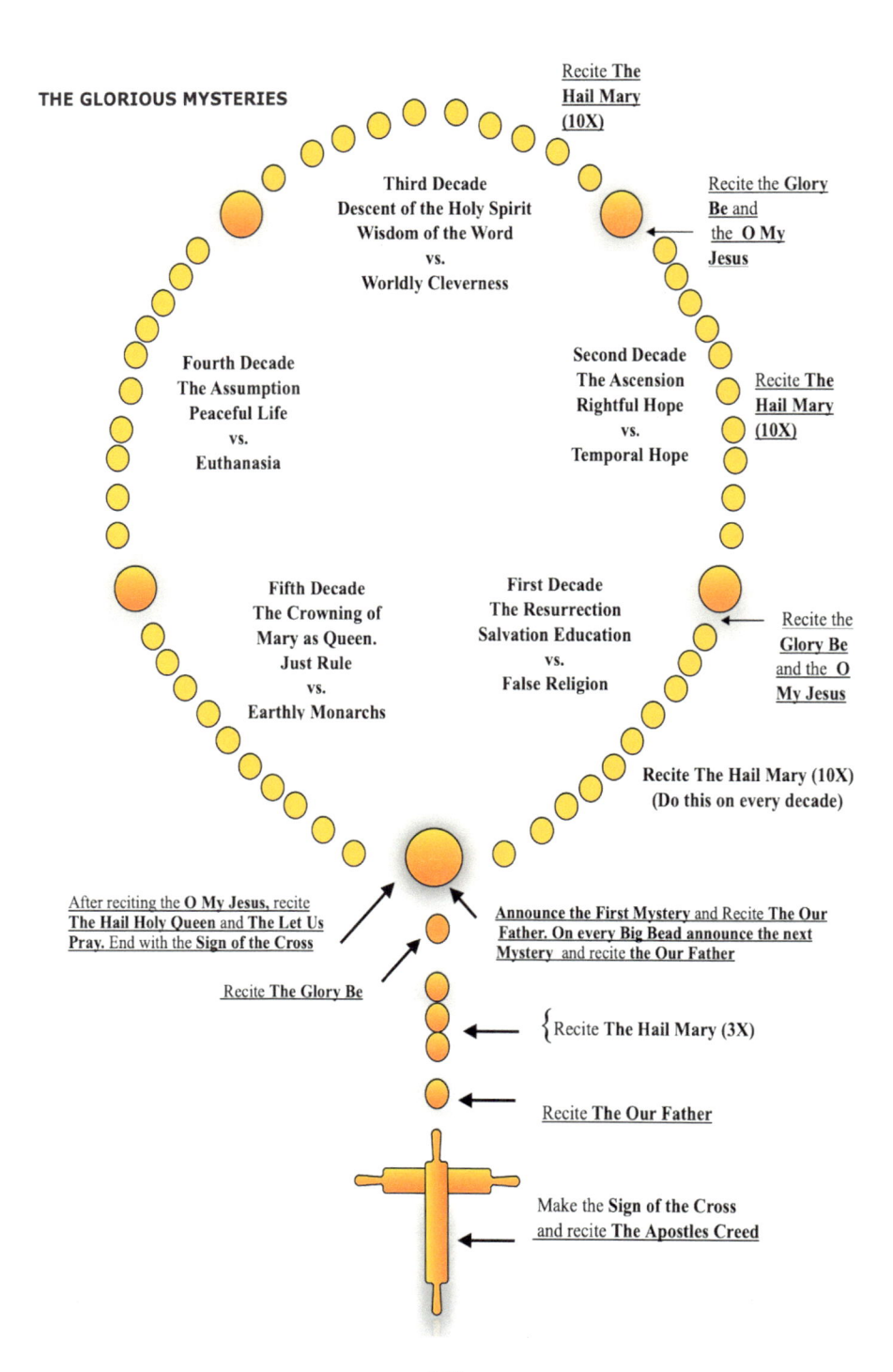

THE GLORIOUS MYSTERIES

Third Decade
Descent of the Holy Spirit
Wisdom of the Word
vs.
Worldly Cleverness

Fourth Decade
The Assumption
Peaceful Life
vs.
Euthanasia

Fifth Decade
The Crowning of
Mary as Queen.
Just Rule
vs.
Earthly Monarchs

Second Decade
The Ascension
Rightful Hope
vs.
Temporal Hope

First Decade
The Resurrection
Salvation Education
vs.
False Religion

Recite **The Hail Mary (10X)**

Recite the **Glory Be** and the **O My Jesus**

Recite **The Hail Mary (10X)**

Recite the **Glory Be** and the **O My Jesus**

Recite The Hail Mary (10X)
(Do this on every decade)

After reciting the **O My Jesus,** recite **The Hail Holy Queen** and **The Let Us Pray.** End with the **Sign of the Cross**

Announce the First Mystery and Recite The Our Father. On every Big Bead announce the next Mystery and recite the Our Father

Recite **The Glory Be**

{ Recite **The Hail Mary (3X)**

Recite **The Our Father**

Make the **Sign of the Cross** and recite **The Apostles Creed**

178

Section Four - Glorious Justice
Chapter One

"Truly we are passing through disastrous times, when we may well make our own, the lamentation of the Prophet: "There is no truth, and there is no mercy, and there is no knowledge of God in the land" (Hosea 4:1). Yet in the midst of this tide of evil, the Virgin Most Merciful rises before our eyes like a rainbow, as the arbiter of peace between God and man."

St. Pius X
(1835-1914)

GLORIOUS MYSTERIES

Justice

What is the cardinal virtue of justice? Rarely does it match the world's definition. Oh, occasionally, there is a just judge, but the essence of justice is the constant and firm will to give their due to God and neighbor. (CCC 1807) Most importantly, well exercised justice always has its ultimate objective in the salvation of souls. It may be punishing, but it is not punitive; it may seem harsh, but it is never excessive; it may risk the reek of a personal vendetta, but it is ever conscious of such possible interpretation and strives to be balanced. Justice always seeks the revelation of the Just One. Justice does not abuse law, natural or wisely manmade. Justice may be appropriately shrewd but never conniving or manipulative. True justice requires a well formed conscience which, in turn is reliant on Knowledge and Understanding, also gifts of the Holy Spirit. Justice seeks truth and goodness—what is right. (CCC 1778)

Justice can be viewed through the Glorious Mysteries. The Just One rose from the dead; He ascended into Heaven and sits at the right hand of the Father. From God the Third Person, the Holy Spirit remains ever ready to assist persons in determining authentic justice. As an advocate is our Blessed Virgin Mother, who was justly assumed into and reigns as Queen of Heaven.

The First Glorious Mystery

The Resurrection (John 20: 1-10)

Virtue: Theological Faith (Knowledge); Salvation Education

Snare: Willful ignorance, denial, or rejection of Knowledge and Understanding

<u>Subject of Contemporary Reflection in God's Light</u>: ***Salvation Education vs. False Religion***

Knowledge with a capital K is an amplification of but distinguished from mere temporal knowledge. Those who possess such knowledge know Holy Scripture and Catechism and are infused with understanding. See the Magisterium of the Church (CCC 85-87) and references to the dogmas of the faith (CCC 88-90). False teaching has its origin in false religion and discordant belief systems that elevate man above God and bend, dissolve, or refigure according to temporal power and its objective.

<u>Model Saint to Know and Imitate</u>: St. Thomas Aquinas was born in 13th century, Italy. This prolific Dominican wrote numerous treatises on the Faith that brought Catholicism to the forefront of critical thinking about faith and reason. His acclaimed Summa of Theology, is one of the most brilliant synthesis of such and of moral and political science, and of Hellenism and Christianity. (*The Pocket Aquinas*, Simon and Schuster, 1960). His many works and superb knowledge

and understanding continues to form minds and support the fundamental doctrine of the Church.

Patti's Stumble Story

Many years ago, I attended a special regional awards luncheon in honor of my late father who had advocated tirelessly for the developmentally disabled. Yet, I, too, had grown in much knowledge and had assisted the primary organization through a regular newsletter, news releases, official documents for governing bodies and agencies, and as a spokesperson. I was most confident in my knowledge and ability to articulate the needs and proposals for this population. I was most happy to expound on the subject, overall.

Others did not necessarily see that in me. As I sat with a group at lunch, I suddenly noticed that I had barely touched my food. A person nearby dryly noted, "That is because you have not stopped talking." Duly chastised, I smiled, maybe laughed in agreement, and made an earnest effort to maintain silence for the rest of the meal.

However, upon reflection, my embarrassment should not have been entirely about my "expertise" in the advocacy and temporal care of the developmentally disabled. I do not recall if I even mentioned I was a teacher at a Catholic school or that my Dad was deeply motivated by his own solid Faith and that he was a Fourth Degree Knight of Columbus —helping to locally start the drive for funding special needs persons; taught Catechism classes twice a week in two different counties; and otherwise, was an outstanding practicing Catholic. It was a missed opportunity. In the political climate of today when the Knights of Columbus are targeted if not vilified as "terrorists," Catholics must ensure they are justly perceived.

Mary's Stumble Story

I worked as an orthopedic medical assistant for sixteen years and then transitioned into the administrative business of healthcare, plaintiff law, and physician training and certification. For almost twenty-six years I did not fully appreciate a patient's perspective of the healthcare system until I became a patient myself—a cancer patient. Suddenly, after my cancer diagnosis, I was introduced to a humbling sense of awareness that being a patient in our healthcare system can be a frightening and impersonal experience.

I was always kind and compassionate to our patients. However, there were days when I was rooming patients, taking blood pressures, taking patient's history, removing sutures or staples from post-surgical sites, and basically moving through my daily schedule in a detached manner. I was physically there, smiling and politely listening to patients, but not truly engaged to the degree I now realize I should have been. In hindsight, I was young, healthy, busy doing paperwork at the station, while all around me patients were in their own heads and bodies trying to cope with pain, unexpected injury, workers' compensation disability issues, fear, sadness, and some were facing their own mortality.

After I went through reconstruction surgeries, two surgical infections, chemotherapy, and more surgeries, becoming a patient truly opened my heart up to understanding a patient's experience in the healthcare setting. Charity champions the Divine call to love and care for our neighbors, especially when they are ill or suffering. God's Petition of Love humbly asks that we see one another as brothers and sisters.

Virtue Narrative

Mary's few lines in Scripture alluded to her being the handmaid of the Lord; anguished puzzlement as to where Jesus was when He was missing for three days, and later, "Do as He tells you" to the wine steward regarding Jesus's first miracle. St. Joseph had no recorded words in Scripture though it is presumed, that as the earthly father, he named Jesus aloud. Even Jesus, being the Creator of all words and the Word, said relatively little when one considers all the books and other communications since the dawn of recorded history.

Knowledge is needed but not a "know it all." As the famous saying goes, "Actions speak louder than words."

The fact is that knowledge with the capital K mandates no one person use his or her human voice, as it is, but that God chooses certain souls to share that Knowledge in many ways. Some would insist most often through silence and martyrdom.

A Contemporary Role Model for this Virtue: Peter Stur

Salvation education requires foremost a knowledge and love of Jesus Christ. One such teacher, a spiritual director and leader of retreats bringing souls to deep immersion in prayer life and a more intimate relationship with Jesus Christ is Peter Stur. Founder of In Ipso (God Within), a Denver-based Catholic ministry (avila-institute.org), Peter has spent decades developing a wholesome but spiritually rich ministry. This mushrooming movement is founded on St. Ignatius's principle of prayers but also includes wisdom from other spiritualities within the Catholic Church. These include Dominican and Carmelite.

Peter's journey resembles many Christians, and it began with more focus on the temporal world. As a youth, Peter Slur was initially eager to fight communism in his native Czechoslovakia, but later he was led to West Germany. There he studies Sacred Scripture, underwent a deep conversion and later immigrated to the United States. Peter, an avid outdoorsman, has been married for 32 years and has ten children. Prior to his devotion to Ipso, he owned and operated a high-end custom kitchen and cabinet design business.

CONVERSION STORY

<u>Dr. Paul Takashi; Eastern Culture Meets Easter Catholicism</u>

Servant of God Dr. Paul Takashi Nagai, born in 1908, survived two major "bombshells" in his life. One was the atomic bomb spawned from dangerous scientific discovery. The other was the spiritual explosion that occurred when this saintly convert joined reason (philosophy) and faith. Although born to a family of some roots in nobility (samurai) and raised in a rural Japanese setting imbued with Confucius and Shinto religion, Paul began a spiritual journey while in medical school. This was prompted by his mother's death. While peering into her eyes, he began to ponder the soul. Later he was introduced to philosophy that would eventually lead him to atheism before coming full circle to Catholicism. He joined the underground church with his wife whose family was one of the driving forces of the persecuted Christian community.

Maximillian Kolbe was among those who personally inspired him in the late 1930s.

Even prior to the fateful blast over Nagasaki, Paul had contracted leukemia from working as a pioneer in radiology research. Yet neither that nor the death of his beloved wife who died in the bombing, stopped him from helping the injured. He was given a reprieve when his cancer mysteriously went into remission for several years.

Later in the spirit of poverty and love, he would reside in a small 6'x6' hovel while caring for his war weary neighbors to whom he brought both physical and spiritual healing. Moreover, he wove texts of forgiveness in articles and best selling book as a legacy for his children and people. Much of this was penned while he lay on his back during the last four years of his life because of the debilitating effects of cancer.

Any earnings went to the education and care of Japanese children orphaned by the war.

His story attracted others, including Helen Keller who traveled to met him. Many people of all faiths and in his country consider Paul Takashi Nagai a saint. Certainly, though a brilliant man, he was a person who actively sought universal truth and became a beacon for the world in the way of simple faith as revealed by the one, holy, Catholic, and apostolic church.

He died on May 1, 1951, at the age of 43, but his legacy lives on.

Rosary Intentions

Petition God that you, spouse, family, neighbors (including perceived enemies or doubters), clergy and religious, educators, health care workers, business persons (including attorneys), politicians (elected, appointed, government employees), public figures (including communicators and entertainers) *seek objective truth and the ability to detect and defeat falsehood.*

THE GLORIOUS MYSTERIES (Mark 16: 1-8; Acts: 1: 6-12; 2: 1-41; Rev. 12)

First Decade *The Resurrection: For the time is coming when people will not endure sound teaching (2 Timothy 4:3-4)* **For: Salvation Education vs False Religion.**

Add a personal faith quote or a prayer intention of your own at the end of this chapter to aid in your meditation:

_____
_____
_____
_____
_____
_____
_____
_____
_____
_____
_____
_____
_____
_____
_____
_____
_____
_____

Helping ourselves and others to **FAITHFULLY** *follow Jesus Christ.*

Section Four - Glorious Justice
Chapter Two

"May God have mercy on you!
May God bless you!
Lord, you know that I am innocent!
With all my heart I forgive my enemies!
Viva Cristo Rey!" he said
shortly before he was executed
by a firing squad for his Catholic faith.

Blessed Miguel Pro
(1891-1927)
Mexican Jesuit & Catholic Martyr
Image of Blessed Miguel Pro kneeling
in prayer minutes before his
execution while holding his rosary.

GLORIOUS MYSTERIES

Justice

Justice and Hope hold hands, as without theological justice, hope for eternal life suffers. Conversely, in the absence of theological hope, justice becomes perverse and strictly punitive in the hands of mankind. The virtue of hope keeps man from discouragement; sustains him during times of abandonment; and opens up his heart in expectation of eternal beatitude. By hope he may be preserved from selfishness and led to the happiness that flows from charity. (CCC 1818). In turn, hope sustains faith. (CCC 162)

The Second Glorious Mystery

The Ascension (Mark 16: 19-20)

Virtue: Theological hope

Snare: Despair or false hope in worldly goods

<u>Subject of Contemporary Reflection in God's Light</u>: ***Rightful Hope vs. Temporal Hope***

Forego temporal reliance on people and things, as they are so *briefly* transitory and lean to the Hope of Heaven. Consider persecutors as *temporary* opponents or oppressors; thieves as those who can only steal material goods; slanderers as those whose reign of defamation will be obliterated by Truth; murderers are those who can kill the body but not the soul.

<u>Model Saint to Know and Imitate</u>: St. Jude is rightfully the patron saint of hopeless causes, but sometimes we limit him to concrete situations and incidents, rather than as an influencer in building up virtue in our souls, the most dynamic for steady faith and generous charity, healing and offering hope.

<u>Patti's Stumble Story</u>

There was a period in my life, I did not want to live. Some thought me suicidal, but in the final analysis of my depressive period, aided by alcohol, I concluded it was not death I was seeking but an escape from the world. It was the temporal life I wanted to end, but because I lacked theological hope…that hope that bases itself on the eternal Word and an everlasting life with God, I was in a quandary. In fact, I had lost faith.

In retrospect, it is easy to acknowledge I actually trusted too much in the world, not just for happiness but also from relief of suffering. A minute could seem forever to someone in mental and spiritual crisis, and a happy ever lasting ending an elusive illusion. That was me. I spent many years thereafter pondering how I arrived at such a state, and I do believe it stemmed from a misunderstanding of all the theological virtues that must be interconnected catechetically to render a cohesive embrace and trust in perfect love.

Today, I can look back and see a person in the throes of doubt and despair. The evil one was nearby through all that turmoil, and that I am now convinced, including "voices." Happily, many prayed for me, and I know I have a strong Guardian Angel. I now view this life as a wonderful gift but not without carrying the cross. Most importantly knowing a greater Gift will follow that no one can destroy or take away. I pray for others now, too, as our world is even more conflicting and discouraging in so many ways. The Guild of St. Benedict Joseph Labre guides me for those who are mentally ill and Encourage for families of loved ones experiencing same sex attraction. Seek first the Kingdom of God and all will be well.

This world is passing away...

<u>Mary's Stumble Story</u>

When I was thirty-four years old and wondering why my father converted to my mother's Catholicism from his 'cradle-faith' which was Judaism, it struck me that the best way to understand Judaism and the Old Testament, was to go directly to the source. So, I began studying the Torah for one year with a Rabbi and her Torah group at a local synagogue. Before I joined the group, I explained to the Rabbi the reason for my interest in studying Torah. The Rabbi kindly let me join the group. I know that in some ways this approach was highly irregular. So irregular, in fact, I did not tell my mother or siblings about my bible group or where it was located. My father had passed away almost ten years earlier at that point in my life. I had religious questions only a Jewish person could answer—or so I thought. Torah means "law." And in this study group a large focus was placed on the five books of Moses: Genesis, Exodus, Leviticus, Numbers, and Deuteronomy. Moses and Abraham are key figures in the Torah, the Old Testament.

I experienced a spiritual roadblock in my Torah study when we began talking about the Word of God and how Jesus is, to the Jewish people, not "The Messiah." The Old Testament describes how the Messiah will arrive, but it stops there; the Jewish people are still waiting for the coming of the Messiah.......

It was at this point in my Torah study that I felt it might be logical to talk about the New Testament with the Torah group. But I was quickly rebuked and immediately shut down by half of the people there. Gently, I was told by the Rabbi that the New Testament contradicts the Old Testament which was divinely inspired by God. Eventually, what I realized about the Torah Study group was this: If it was just a matter of explaining who Jesus Christ truly is, and I had full theological knowledge of the Old and New Testament on my side, then everybody would immediately convert—everybody would be Christian! But, it doesn't matter how much you know about your own faith or how much people cling to their faith. There must be a moment of spiritual conversion for that individual person; an illumination of conscience. And until that person is ready, until the Holy Spirit is present within them, there's nothing another person can do to change somebody's state of mind or reality. Of course, we can faithfully bring Jesus to the modern world where we can, but the Holy Spirit must be there to open their ears and uncover their eyes.

<u>Virtue Narrative</u>

The following is from Magnificat, August 2023, within a beautiful editorial by Father Sebastian White, O.P. He quotes Father Farrell, a beloved Dominican who died in 1951. He suggests "replacing" Dominican with Catholic, as it is true for both.

"Let God tend to the hopeless-looking things. You are a Dominican, a foreigner to worry and a close friend of gaiety. It seems to me quite entrancing to be able to pile into bed realizing there is someone as big as God to do all the worrying that has to be done. Worry, you know, is a kind of reverence given to a situation because of its magnitude; how small it must be through God's eyes. You can't get everything done in a day, nor can you get any part of it done as well as it could be, or even as well as you'd like it; so, like the rest o us, you putter at your job with a normal amount of energy, for a reasonable length of time, and go to bed with the humiliating yet exhilarating knowledge that you are only a child of God and not God himself."

A Contemporary Role Model for this Virtue: Timothy Duff

Perhaps the greatest obstacle to growing in Faith in the midst of the tremendous cultural battles all around us is the false sense that we "should be doing something (Catholic), and that something must be "loud, continuous, and assertive" to stop the madness. We must remain a people of trust and hope even while conscientiously defending Truth. When tempted to grow exasperated with the inability to even speak out, at times, or seem to make any impression on the mushrooming evil, we must always recognize that we are not the "solution," but the Faithful.

Most people do not know Timothy Duff, co-founder of the Guild of St. Benedict Joseph Labre for those with mental illness and brain disorders, regardless of cause. With his late mother, Mildred, and the counsel of Father Benedict Joseph Groeschel, the Guild grew from hundreds of "kitchen table letters" from 1996 forward to several thousand families over the decades. In addition to individual family members, the Guild attracted the spiritual adoption by nearly four hundred religious communities.

Timothy became a Catholic Lay hospital chaplain and also worked for the Massachusetts Department of Mental Health. Today, this widower with two daughters remains an active advocate and leads almost daily ZOOM prayer for members. His three brothers suffer(ed) from schizophrenia or mental illness. Tim's guardianship over the most severely impacted, Scott, institutionalized most of his adult life, only recently ended when this once identified "good candidate for euthanasia" passed by natural causes on August 24, 2024.

CONVERSION STORY

Saint Josephine Bahkita

When this work was first drafted, persons were included who had converted in the 19th to 20th century, assuming some would be saints. Saint Josephine Bahkita was one who was canonized in recent times even as this draft sat in a binder for years. We include her as a sign of hope for us all.

Born around 1869 in Darfur, Sudan, St. Josephine Bakhita knew the horrors of child abuse, slavery, and later religious persecution. At age nine, she was kidnapped by slave traders and beaten bloody, then sold five times in the slave markets of Sudan. Eventually, she worked as a slave for the mother and wife of a general, but was flogged daily, impressing upon her body 144 scars for the remainder of her life. (Ponder that number.) Finally, in 1882 (the year our grandmother was born on an idyllic farm in Osage, Iowa), an Italian merchant bought her for the Italian consul Callisto Legnani, who returned to Italy.

It was here that Josephine would surrender to the true "Master" though totally different from the terrifying ones she had known previously. She used the name "paron" for this Master, the living God, the God of Jesus Christ. In one depiction of her life there is a flashback to her witnessing a crucifixion as a child, so when Josephine saw the Cross, she embraced the Suffering Jesus. She grew in love of him, knowing how much He loved her. Now she had hope, a hope that extended beyond the world to eternity: "I am definitely loved and whatever happens to me —I am awaited by this Love. And so my life is good." Through this hope she was "redeemed," no longer a slave, but a free child of God. She had a deep understanding of Ephesians and the theme of hope St. Paul presented. This gave her strength to resist a return to Sudan who did not wish to be separated from her "Paron."

On January 9, 1890, she was baptized and confirmed and received her first Communion from the hands of the Patriarch of Venice. In 1896, in Verona, after a legal battle, she was emancipated and took her vows in the Congregation of the Canossian Sisters taking on the modest work of a sacristan and in the porter's lodge at the convent. She promoted missions around Italy spreading her message of liberating hope that she had received in her encounter with Jesus Christ.

Of course, none of the blessings she received negates the inexcusable manner in which she was degraded much of her life. Still, St. Josephine Bahkita brings to the world the Truth, and that Truth is always bound in Perfect Love that transcends all injustice.

Rosary Intentions

Pray that you, spouse or close friend, family, neighbors (including perceived enemies or doubters), religious and clergy, educators, health care workers, business persons (including attorneys), politicians (elected, appointed, government employees), public figures (including communicators and entertainers) *distinguish between earthly hope and theological hope and be uplifted towards an eternal destination despite what appears hopeless in this world.*

THE GLORIOUS MYSTERIES (Mark 16: 1-8; Acts: 1: 6-12; 2: 1-41; Rev. 12)

Second Decade *The Ascension:* *We put our hope in the Lord; He is our help and our shield. (Psalm 33:20)* **For Rightful Hope vs Temporal Hope.**

Add a personal faith quote or a prayer intention of your own at the end of this chapter to aid in your meditation:

_____
_____
_____
_____
_____
_____
_____
_____
_____
_____
_____
_____
_____
_____
_____
_____
_____
_____
_____

Helping ourselves and others to **FAITHFULLY** *follow Jesus Christ.*

Section Four - Glorious Justice
Chapter Three

"Gratitude is the first sign
of a thinking, rational creature."

Blessed Solanus Casey
(1870-1957)

GLORIOUS MYSTERIES

Justice

Perfect Justice embodies perfect love, and honor is the social witness which is given to human dignity. Thus detraction and calumny offend against the virtues of justice and charity. (CCC 2479). This relates to the pursuit of wisdom and against false teaching, as others belief systems do not uphold personhood in the same high regard as Catholicism. Catholicism uplifts, whereas other religions often hype focus on secular surroundings which leads to temptation to sin against one's neighbor even in the name of being "righteous." Justice, on the other hand ensures that all children of God, regardless of politics and other social labels, receive that birthright. We must all seek what is right and good even when decisions are difficult and moral judgments less assured. (CCC 1787) In modern times, the Holy Spirit, who is honored by several names, exposes the world's ruses. (CCC 1433, 692, 1848, 2466).

The Third Glorious Mystery

The Descent of the Holy Spirit (Acts 2: 1-13)

Virtue: Pursuit of wisdom

Snare: Gnosticism and other heresies

<u>Subject of Contemporary Reflection in God's Light</u>: **Wisdom of the World vs. Worldly Cleverness**

We are challenged to discern authentic wisdom and distinguish it from the intellectualism of the world and arrive at Truth that is shared in love. Yet, it is no easy road while navigating through assaults from all sides. (See Chapter Three—CCC 683-747)

Model Saint to Know and Imitate: *The Imitation of Christ*, St. Thomas Kempis's classic fifteenth century work on how to be Christ like, has been noted as one of the most important devotional approaches to living a holy life. Often found next to the Bible, this scriptural based counsel has led millions of Christians along a dependable path. Its author, a respected Augustine monk, born into poverty, soon became a disciple of piety. Also known for his sermons on the life and passion of Jesus Christ, prayers, and mediations, Kempis of the Netherlands showed a knack for stirring the conscience of his readers—and still does—but remained himself the humble disciple of his own spiritual directives. His work has been published in numerous languages and over the centuries many times over. Even Moody, the Protestant sect, published this work that included the Eucharist.

Patti's Stumble Story

The young Democrats sat in a circle around then state legislator Leo McCarthy, a Catholic, and listened with attentive minds to his wisdom about the politics of the day. Leo McCarthy was a sincere man and genuinely sought to educate youth on current societal issues and needs and how to meet them with clarity and determination. It was not unusual for him or other California Democrats in the early 70s to invite us into their homes or at least homey settings to discourse and "guide."

At the time, I recall the sense of belonging but more, the confidence that we could solve poverty and injustice. I experienced a trust in these persons, many of whom did sacrifice personally for what they believed. This was not the Democrat Party of 2024, but the red flags, literally, were flying. I witnessed that first hand, and the political climate of the day was not as corrupt as now. Now, I hasten to interject that not all Democrats or politicians were so well intended. I remember one candidate for whom I pounded the payment only to see him have to withdraw due a scandalous affair with an underage girl. And, some were better than others. Still, there was not the spirit of intense antagonism as today.

Additionally, the professors in my studies in the area of political science were providing sufficient kudos to my analyses. Again, though, strict expectations were in place. On one occasion, following a car accident, I had to "settle" for a "B" in a course, as I then was compelled to submitted a late paper. Later that teacher exclaimed that he would have given me an "A" had he had the paper before grades were due. Ahhh, flattery. As balance, not all papers were so well scored.

Yet, I was wholly wrong to place so much trust in human endeavors and evaluations. Even while attending these meetings, brainstorming, and contributing time and talent (no treasure then) to advancing their careers, I attended Mass, but do not recall ever asking the Holy Spirit to guide me. I was a ritualistic Catholic at the time and way too dependent on the world to solve our messes. Besides many of these politicians were Catholic, or at least Christian.

Eventually, almost without exception, everyone in politics would disappoint me with their various falls from grace. None disappointed me more than...me.

Mary's Stumble Story

After receiving my paralegal studies certificate from my alma mater, St. Mary's College, I was interested in combining my healthcare experience with my legal education. When I went to interview for a law library position, I quickly discovered this position was not in the main law library at the Hall of Justice but the law library which was housed inside the jail—next door to the Hall of Justice! This was not advertised as a "jail law library" position. After three rounds of panel interviews and a background investigation, I was selected for the position.

Working with 'clients' who are incarcerated is a difficult task. Many of the crimes these inmates were accused of committing rendered some insight into the human psyche which can be virtually imprisoned by darkness and vice. This jail environment demanded that the Catholic in me suspend judgement on another human being. I continually told myself to focus on the reason why we provide case law and books to those who are in jail and accused of a crime(s). Also, remembering to focus NOT on the gravity of their alleged crime(s) but on the fact that each one of these individuals was created in the image of God. As a human being, this is a difficult ask.

How could God ask me to love these as my brother or sister? God knew each of them... what they did....yet it was so hard for me not to 'judge' their actions. All the while clinging to the wisdom that I should do this job well—trust and do God's work. Which is not to say I could turn my physical back on an inmate for a second! Even when I had to go into the higher security modules for those inmates who were not allowed to be among the general population in the jail library, my life was always at risk. The energy in male inmate modules is foreboding and tense. While they await their trial dates they are pacing, nervous, and agitated. Many of these inmates were hardened criminals who simply wanted to get out again, at any cost. How I helped these individuals is still a mystery to me. When asked at the completion of my 18 month assignment by the Sheriff's Department if I would seriously like to consider a position as a Correctional Officer, I responded with a respectful, "No, thank you."

Narrative Virtue

Tension is ever present between even moral leadership and supernatural authority. President Bush and many others sounded the drumbeat against mass weapons in the Middle East, particularly Iraq. His almost visceral dislike of Saddam Hussein, perhaps due to avenging his father, struck many as concerning. However, it appeared that a preventive action was necessary. What followed was disastrous. What most sticks in our memory of that fiasco, a war that should not have been launched was Pope John Paul II's warning against it. His calm but firm admonishment against invading Iraq still resonates with many Catholics today. Here was the ideal combination of political savvy and wisdom, and the words and works of this great Pope should be a lesson taught in all history classes. Most assuredly, St. Pope John Paul II entreated the Holy Spirit continuously and persistently.

A Contemporary Role Model for this Virtue: Sister Miriam James Heidland

Sister Miriam James Heidland (SOLT—Society of Our Lady of the Most Holy Trinity) under went a radical conversion—some would say reversion—to the Catholic Faith after living in the world for a time as a popular athlete and attractive young woman. Featured on EWTN's "The Journey Home" this vibrant nun is often sought for talks regarding her leaving the world and responding to a call to religious life. She holds a master's in theology from the Augustine Institute, but it is her dynamic speaking presence that captivates audiences of all ages, particularly the young.

Yet, what may set her apart from others is her stark, unreserved admittance to a past replete with darkness, shame, and addiction. She proclaims the power of personal witness and that this can move others in the direction towards a genuinely loving relationship with Jesus Christ. Whereas before sports was one of her deepest loves, she transformed that to the love of the race, as in St. Paul's exhortation to "run so as to win." (1 Cor 9:24). She employed the same discipline and training towards building her Faith life.

Sister Miriam works on the motto of "at the heart of every person, every person longs for communion and relationship."

St. Joan of Arc exhibited the type of boldness that appeals to Sister Miriam, who claims she is actually shy and quiet. She asserts that we need such female witnesses in the world, those who are willing to spiritually fight and suffer. The enthusiastic disciple continues her work to transform the world to those things that are most important.

CONVERSION STORY

Creighton Abrams

At first glance, it might seem odd to highlight the conversion of a Vietnam era general, Creighton Abrams, while contemplating the Descent of the Holy Spirit. Yet, who else so stirred this famous general and other military personnel through history, even in the Bible?

Creighton was the son of a railroad repair man but graduated from West Point and continued in a brilliant military career that placed him as a peer to World War II George Patton. There was even a tank named after the boisterous, cigar smoking military leader, the "M1 Abrams".

Although his military career landed the General in the controversial Vietnam War between 1968 and 1972, it was also during his tenure there that he embraced Roman Catholicism. General Abrams died of lung cancer at the age of 59 while Army Chief of Staff. His wife, Julie, who was known for her humanitarian efforts was later buried with him at Arlington Cemetery.

Parenthetically, we can add that our own father, Colonel Harold Sobel, a convert from Judaism in the early 1940's served under General Abrams twice, in addition to serving under General Walter T. Kerwin, another staunchly devout Catholic. Our father was a devotee of the Sacred Heart and carried a small metal badge with the image of the Sacred Heart in his uniform pocket along with a picture of the Blessed Mother holding the infant Jesus, as well.

General Kerwin's association with General Abrams in Vietnam between 1968 and 1970 may well have also impacted the former Methodist. Although highly decorated and the person responsible for ending the draft as we know it, General Kerwin most esteemed a Papal Medal conferred on him by a Cardinal, a distinction engraved on his headstone in Arlington Cemetery.

These are only a few notable Catholic military men who worked tirelessly to defend our country, in some small part for the freedoms we enjoy, including religious freedom. Though not responsible for the forces that brought our world to war, they remained courageous and ethical and never wavered in their allegiance to this country and God.

Today, we are facing significant challenges to those freedoms, but we can ask for the intercession of the soldiers who have gone before us, before the throne of God. May we earnestly seek that wisdom of the Holy Spirit to guide us to effective peaceful means to bring souls to salvation.

Rosary Intentions

Pray that you, a spouse or close friend, family, neighbors (including perceived enemies or doubters, clergy and religious, educators, health care workers, business persons (including attorneys), politicians (elected, appointed, government employees), public figures (including communicators and entertainers) doubters *seek the Holy Spirit frequently during the day and for the night and act on the promptings.*

THE GLORIOUS MYSTERIES (Mark 16: 1-8; Acts: 1: 6-12; 2: 1-41; Rev. 12)

Third Decade *The Descent of the Holy Spirit: All wisdom is from the Lord, and Wisdom is with him forever. (Sirach 1:1)* **For: Wisdom of the Word vs Worldly Cleverness.**

Add a personal faith quote or a prayer intention of your own at the end of this chapter to aid in your meditation:

_____
_____
_____
_____
_____
_____
_____
_____
_____
_____
_____
_____
_____
_____
_____
_____
_____
_____

*Helping ourselves and others to **FAITHFULLY** follow Jesus Christ.*

Section Four - Glorious Justice
Chapter Four

"WHAT DOES IT MATTER TO YOU WHETHER JESUS
WISHES TO GUIDE YOU TO HEAVEN
BY WAY OF THE DESERT OR BY THE MEADOW,
SO LONG AS HE IS ALWAYS WITH YOU
AND YOU ARRIVE AT THE POSSESSION
OF A BLESSED ETERNITY?"
PADRE PIO

GLORIOUS MYSTERIES

JUSTICE

The position of a justice of the peace originated in England in 1361 (encyclopedia.com) As its name implies, this lower level magistrate was assigned to basically keep the peace, maintaining community order. Offenses included many of the sins denounced by the Ten Commandments. However perfect justice promises an eternal peace where justice will be inherently and indelibly impressed upon all souls. (CCC 769) The challenge is to emulate the just person in this life to experience peace even in the midst of suffering, as oxymoronic as that seems. However, the closer earthly justice is to the ideal, the greater the peace even on Earth. All are responsible for realizing the common good…to promote institutions that improve the condition of human life. (CCC 1917)

The Fourth Glorious Mystery

The Assumption of Mary into Heaven (Declared by the Church)

Virtue: Peaceful Life Amid Suffering

Snare: Disturbance and Unfounded Fear; Killing Life before Natural Death

<u>Subject of Contemporary Reflection in God's Light</u>: ***Peaceful Life and Death vs. Suicide and Euthanasia***

How our grasp of the reality of Mary's Assumption into Heaven, Body and Soul informs our daily lives and orders us to peace and trust. Suicide and euthanasia not only deprive a person of many graces for self and others, but may end badly for eternity, though we may not judge the state of anyone's soul at death.

<u>Model Saint to Know and Imitate</u>: No human being was so blessed as Mary, the Mother of Jesus Christ, but no man or woman suffered so intensely as she either from the moment of the Incarnation. Moreover, several mystics agree that Mary had fore knowledge of her Son's ultimate passion and crucifixion. Seven times a Sorrowful sword pierced her heart, and four of those were along the way or under the Cross. However, at all times Mary exhibited an extraordinary presence of serenity and love. For she also knew of the Resurrection and the life to come. So her intercession for any persons dying for any reason is most powerful. (CCC 2299)

<u>Patti's Stumble Story</u>

Here would be a good site to focus on "peace in death," and St. Joseph is the Patron Saint of a peaceful death. Yet, it would be in my later years that I would fully appreciate this. I never gave much thought or prayer to Mary's Assumption though the Rosary was often included in my Catholic schooling and particularly during the Crowning of Mary. Still, contemplating that Mary's body, mind, and soul never underwent corruption was a more senior moment.

Herein, though I am being led to focus on what tears apart the person more than any other assault, and that is despairing anger that impacts brain chemistry, erodes the soul, and actually attacks the body. I have thought of myself as a "victim" of a corrupt society, as a woman, wife, and mother.

After being almost murderously attacked decades ago by a male companion of a "liberated" female friend who had abandoned me at a club, I would be so traumatized by her turncoat viciousness as to forgo female friendships for years. Later as a wife of a divorced father, I witnessed grave injustices against fathers by city prosecutors and state law. As a mother of a child with special needs, it seemed that the health machine, hamstrung by major insurance companies, and education institutions were completely politicalized and anti-family. In all, I was in a disturbed place of mind. My intellect succumbed to my passions; my imagination took me to the worst scenarios than were actually experienced.

The resentful anger I vented was not only unChristian, it must have grieved Our Lady and Heavenly Mother who never raised her voice but rested peacefully in the will of God. Unlike me, as well, Mary was completely innocent, a true victim, while I had erred in many ways as a woman, wife and mother.

Certainly, there was a genuine sense of injustice, a satisfaction in the "fight," and even celebration over short term victories. Still, throughout the trials and tribulations, I was left empty for the most part.

It has taken many decades to arrive at the posture I hope to present privately and publicly which is to focus on that which is killing souls and avoiding defaming any person, even those responsible for the catastrophic consequences for our cultural—moral—health.

In private prayer, just last night, it has been impressed on me that all these persons are children of God, and He does not want to lose even one to the evil one. It is our duty to persevere and even suffer for that end. What was more startling was the message that I would be held personally accountable for any person I discouraged and dissuaded from Truth, even when thinking I was acting on behalf of Truth. Anger is a killer, more so than injustice because we cannot always control injustice, but we (I) can control (our) my response to it.

Still, a distinction must be made. I have numerous personal anecdotes that attest to our Catholic duty to cite public figures acting in spiritually dangerous ways against the public.

<u>Mary's Stumble Story</u>

As a student of a Catholic college I was exposed to the concepts of theology, Christian citizenship, and the intellectually disciplined process of critical thinking. Knowing that by courageously opening doors once shut to strangers, a person can become a bridge which can lead to better cultural understanding. For me, a key role model for developing a broader world view was Mother Teresa. She was a bridge between two worlds; building goodwill and charity, person by person; she was an example of how to lay a groundwork of charity which led her to creating peaceful solutions and building gentle pathways to break down various stigmas and cultural differences in our world.

My hope for humanity has been challenged by social influences which have left me feeling less than optimistic about peace. For example, why would a group of people live in a culture that glorifies Death? Why would humanity choose to build up its nuclear capabilities under the guise of "brokering peace" and by doing so offer to formulate a "nuclear agreement" out of it? That concept appears counterintuitive, as opposed to laying down weapons to broker a proper peace. The horrors of the atomic age during World War II, or the Holocaust, has not stopped human aggression or pure hatred.

The darkness that roams this earth is looking to deliver Death, not Life. Clearly, Evil glorifies Death. Many have monstrously deformed human death into a glorification pact that aligns with the freedom to choose abortion and the freedom to commit suicide. This pact is branded as a social resistance to oppression. Only Evil can spin this kind of mockery, create war and horrible violence, so that it can celebrate death over and over, feed on it, gain power from it, fuel political campaigns with it, and then call this gross machination some kind of Freedom Movement.

It is with great despair that I admit I am discouraged with Humanity! My own human emotions come spilling out at times when I should remain silent. I have been praying to understand why God wants us to love and care for our enemies, Evil incarnate, as it continues on a path mercilessly killing everyone in its way. Suicidal ideology only mocks Christ's Passion and benevolent sacrifice for all of us. I struggle with this mockery every day. God help me to remember that you are asking me to pray for my enemies' conversion and for those living in the darkness of underground tunnels and other dark places, so that they will come to find you, love you and pray for your Divine Mercy.

<u>Virtue Narrative</u>

There is no greater illustration of the ultimate Assumption of Mary than the very virtuous manner in which Mary lived her life from birth. There is no doubt that Mary heeded all directions in her self care and in submitting to anyone else's care for her body, from childhood. There is every indication that despite poverty, she and St. Joseph were always fed sufficiently for their health, that she followed the dictates of the Law in purification, and ever maintained a presence of cleanliness.

Every image of Mary demonstrates a robust physical appearance that nearly glows…is translucent. Although this may be more enhanced following her Assumption, it can be certain that she always had a flushed complexion and bright eyes, reflecting a well balanced lifestyle that also lent itself to great vigor, at times, like her trek to see Elizabeth, even while pregnant. Mary had not only physical stamina but an even emotional balance. She exuded intelligence and the development of habits that maintained health for an extraordinary journey in life, especially preparing her for the Passion and Crucifixion of her Son, Jesus Christ.

How she must look upon our world with great sorrow as her beautiful children choose contraception and abortion—children are murdered in the womb; developing youth are mutilated and left in despair with deformed bodies and abandoned souls; and euthanasia bodes poorly for the despairing. She weeps at our indifference to the marginalized, the genuinely oppressed migrant, and the disabled. However, she also pleads for her sons and daughters in the grip of illusion about what is truly good and true.

Mary, conceived without sin, in the full bloom of life from this world to the next, pray for us who have recourse to thee.

A Contemporary Role Model for this Virtue: Renee Bondi

Her life was peaking with a wonderful singing voice, a terrific music teaching job and fiancé. At 29, though, that would all change when a freakish accident—an awkward dreamlike tumble from her bed—would leave Renee paralyzed from the neck down. Told she would never sing again, and though the previously energetic woman would endure months of recovery and adaptation to her extremely limited situation, Renee nonetheless vowed to retrain her vocal cords. Fortunately the man of her dreams stood by. She proved the experts wrong and built a music company; presented as a motivational speaker at many events, often Christian, and even enjoyed childbirth which gave her a son.

Renee could have simply given up after her accident. Today, she may have been prompted to "die with dignity." But those were never an option. The confident woman attributes much of her confidence and hope to her Faith, but it was also an understanding of the preciousness of life. Though she would no longer be in command of her body, many other "hands" would help. With grace, Renee today has inspired millions to accept suffering but with joyful anticipation.

CONVERSION STORY

Casey Jones: From Railway Worker to Religious Ways

As the story goes, the fabled railroad hero, Casey Jones, fell head over heels in love with a young Catholic girl, and he converted to please her. Even so, by all accounts, Casey was a devoted husband and father of three children known for his teetotaler ways and was highly respected by peers.

Now, in those days—the late 1800s—railroad work was highly dangerous. Trains did not have sophisticated electrical systems for flexibility and quick response. One of Casey's positions was a brakeman, an exceedingly risky task as it required balance, coordination, and intense concentration, particularly on inclines and as when a train descended around curves on the tracks. Possibly due to a yellow fever outbreak that dwindled the railroad workers population, Casey achieved a lifelong dream of becoming an engineer. He gained a reputation as a punctual "driver" who would go to great lengths to run the trains as advertised and transport freight to its destination on time. However, that did cost him numerous infraction citations as he was somewhat of a daredevil, too. He was also known for his particular whistle, the sound of which people could recognize from their beds.

Yet, one of his crowning achievements was transporting people to the famous World Exposition of 1893 in Chicago. He was also praised for saving a little girl from the tracks once in Mississippi in a daring grab for the scared stiff youngster from the front end cowcatcher—so named as trains could bump into errant cattle. The avid baseball fan would meet his fate in a horrible train accident that would cost his life on April 30, 1900. He was almost immediately heralded for his bravery to stop the train before hitting a stalled caboose, likely shrouded in the foggy and rainy night. Since that time, his name has been synonymous with the Iron Bronco days, and he has been immortalized in song and stamps. He rode the rails, embracing life, and finding God's amazing grace on the tracks that would end at the final station.

Rosary Intentions
===

As we meditate on this Mystery, let us pray that you, a spouse, family, neighbors (including perceived enemies or doubters), clergy and religious, educators and health care workers, business persons (including attorneys), politicians (elected, appointed, government employees, public confused. figures (including communicators and entertainers) *embrace Truth and provide others the promise of a natural, peaceful death. Ask for the protection of life and assistance for the confused.*

THE GLORIOUS MYSTERIES (Mark 16: 1-8; Acts: 1: 6-12; 2: 1-41; Rev. 12)

Fourth Decade *The Assumption of Mary, Mother of God:* *The Christian who dies in Christ Jesus is 'away from the body and at home with the Lord'. (2 For 5:8 CCD 1681)* **For: Peaceful Life and Death vs Self-Inflicted Death and Euthanasia.**

Add a personal faith quote or a prayer intention of your own at the end of this chapter to aid in your meditation:

_____
_____
_____
_____
_____
_____
_____
_____
_____
_____
_____
_____
_____
_____
_____

*Helping ourselves and others to **FAITHFULLY** follow Jesus Christ.*

Section Four - Glorious Justice
Chapter Five

In a final letter written only a few hours before Mother Teresa died on 5 September 1997, she wrote: "We have much to thank God for, especially that He has given us Our Lady's spirit to be the spirit of our Society. Loving Trust and Total Surrender made Our Lady say "Yes" to the message of the angel, and Cheerfulness made her to run in haste to serve her cousin Elizabeth. That is so much of our life, saying "Yes" to Jesus and running in haste to serve Him…"

Saint Teresa of Calcutta
(1910-1997)

GLORIOUS MYSTERIES

Justice

Mary is Queen of Heaven and Earth, for all eternity, and sits by Jesus Christ, the Just One. Yet, while on Earth, Mary also exemplified that virtue, most impressibly in the Magnificat, but also in daily life. ("Mary and Justice", Father Johann Rosen, S.M., udayton.edu). Mary led the way to re-establish the initial harmony as when there was a state between the first couple and all creation called "original justice." (CCC 376) From the Annunciation to the Assumption, Mary always accepted God's righteousness through faithfulness in Jesus Christ. Righteousness (or justice) here means the rectitude of Divine love. With justification faith, hope, and charity were poured into Mary's heart, and obedience to the divine will was granted her—which can be the same for each of us. (CCC 387 and 1991)

The Fifth Glorious Mystery

The Crowning of Mary as Queen of Heaven and Earth (Revelations: 12: 1-5)

Virtue: Reverence for the True Queen; authentic Royalty

Snare: Disrespect of that which is Holy Womanhood

Subject of Contemporary Reflection in God's Light: ***Just Rule vs. Earthly Monarchy***

Mary is Queen of both the temporal world and heaven; she is the true and most loving royalty aside from and beside her Son, Jesus Christ, the King. She is the Queen Mother. We are her princesses (daughters) and princes (sons).

<u>Model Saint(s) to Know and Imitate</u>: The great kings and queens in history who lived sanctified lives while ruling temporal kingdoms: St. Helena, St. Clotilde, St. Adelaide, St. Elizabeth of Portugal, St, Jadwiga of Poland, Bl. Maria Cristina of Savoy. St. Edward the Confessor, St. Louis IX of France, St. Ferdinand III of Castile, St. Stephen of Hungary, and King Henry II. Furthermore, there were many holy examples of monarchy who lived with great charity but ruled efficiently and effectively.

<u>Patti's Stumble Story</u>

Now, I had a deep love of Mary, Mother of Jesus Christ, throughout my childhood, and I never brazenly disrespected her even at a distance from my Faith. However, from leaping to near expectation of visions during childhood May Crownings to my college years, at some point, I merely began avoiding her.

Then in the late 1960s, I focused more on the world, and it was drag queens who captivated my imagination. At that time, I was engrossed in the glitz of San Francisco, and North Beach was a magnet for those seeking these novel entertainers. They looked eerily like beauty models, some with figures many women would have envied. When I gazed upon the heavy make up and dynamic dresses, and watched their smooth moves or listened to nicely voiced song, I even felt some jealousy. They were having a lot more fun than I, while earning some serious money. Not once do I recall considering the conflict of their lifestyle with Faith.

Of course, my imagined position of royalty would be more typical. I would have preferred to be like the Queen of Sheba. Still, if I were honest, like many girls I fantasized about the proverbial Prince Charming who would lead me to riches and a life of ease and prestige.

So, for too many years, the world drew me, not towards the Cross but away from it, and therefore, away from Mary who cannot stand close to hubris.

Ironically, it would be much later that I learned about the Sheba I envied, and in actuality, despite her fame and beauty, she would hold Truth to be the greatest possession and pursuit. One perspective in christianity.com *notes that the Queen of Sheba traveled about 1,500 miles seeking wisdom from Solomon may well be a model for today as "the world seeks wisdom in academia, social leaders, politicians, the evening news and even psychics.*

I would have done much better had I known of Sheba more thoroughly (1 Kings 10:1-2 and 2 Chronicles 9:1-13.) I also imagine that Sheba would have been a deep admirer of the Blessed Virgin Mary and curtsied to her.

Mary's Stumble Story

It has taken me years to put my Catholic faith back together in a way which is less choppy in its discernment. Admittedly, I am a slow, religious kind of forever-student when it comes to understanding the depth of scripture and God's love for me. More of my time should have been spent talking with my children about God, the Holy Family, the

Blessed Mother, and why His presence in this world is so necessary in their daily life. Especially now! So many missed moments of faithful clarity and peace for my children were traded off due to worldly distractions.

My greatest understanding of God's love for me came when I was in despair a few years ago. You see, I am the living example of the Samaritan woman who met Jesus at the well. My first marriage was annulled, a civil marriage failed, and when I married again in 2004, I did not marry in the church. For almost twenty years I was unable to receive communion. I was an 'outcast' in my faith, an 'outcast' in the church, without the body and blood of Christ in my life. Until a few years ago....when a personal miracle happened to me!

I was in my loft on the computer when all of a sudden I stopped typing...put my head in my hands and spontaneously began crying—full sobbing. As my tears began dropping one after another onto the floor, an overwhelming feeling of grief and surrender enveloped my body and soul. What was I doing all this for? My personal, earthly goals were suddenly and completely meaningless. My spiritual emptiness became palpable and physically painful in that moment. In the middle of all of my sobbing, I told Jesus I missed Him so much, was so hungry and thirsty after walking in this desert of shame and loneliness without Him by my side. But ...why would He console me, a blundering sinner? And what did the word 'Beloved' really mean.... ? I had read that word in the Bible the night before. I did not know what "Beloved" meant when Jesus said this word to His people. Nor did I feel worthy of being loved for all I had done in my life which outwardly appeared to reject the sacrifices He made for me.

In deep emotional pain, sitting in my computer chair sobbing, I heard a voice say to me in my head, "You thirst for the living water.

You hunger for the bread of life. You, Mary, ARE my BELOVED. You have always been...but love yourself as I love you! Come back to my house and receive me. Marry in the church. Do what you need to do...but back come home to Me! I am here for you right now!"

As this warm feeling came over me and filled my body head to toes with love and parental embrace, I became aware of the presence of the Holy Spirit. I leaned over my desk to grab my favorite pen in the pencil holder so I could write down what I was experiencing and hearing. As I pulled the pen from the pencil holder something very small and red was stuck under the pen clip.

As I pulled what was stuck to the pen clip and looked at it, I was stunned. It was a very small, red rectangle cardboard sticker and it had white lettering—just one word was printed on it. It said: **BELOVED**.

You have to know that I have never purchased a tiny cardboard sticker like this, and my pencil holder only contains pens and pencils. Where did this prophetic 'gift' come from? I believe it is a private miracle. A tangible love message from Jesus, whom I will love to my death with all my heart. It is a tangible piece of His love for me to treasure and to hold! For I am His Beloved. I am His child, and He truly loves me after all I have failed to do. His love never fails us!

Within a matter of six months, my husband and I had a convalidation ceremony in the church, in front of our congregation. I received Holy Communion for the first time in nineteen years! When I did receive communion after all that time without Him, I thought I was going to faint right there in front of the altar for I was so overwhelmed with joy, love, belonging, welcoming, and life.... His life in me. That day, I felt that if I was to die right there at the altar, my life would have been serenely complete. Thank you, sweet Shepherd, for bringing me back to your flock. And bringing my husband back, which is another miracle, too!

Virtue Narrative

The Queen of Heaven—She was a quiet, hidden young lady when the angel appeared to her, and she responded not with "Oh, so I am to be the Mother of God"? But "I am the handmaiden of the Lord." Then she proceeded to walk the same path of poverty and suffering of Our Lord Jesus Christ. Her—Queen of Heaven—knew from her Son's infancy that a sword would pierce her own heart. Her Royalty—had to flee to a foreign country because of the cruel leadership by one of her own in the Jewish faith. Mary, soon to reign over all children, had to fret about a missing Son. Mary, to be forever crowned in Heaven had to bear seeing Jesus Christ wear a crown of thorns and His scourged body crucified. She held Him in her arms afterwards, not unlike the mothers whose children are battered in our streets or otherwise marginalized in our society for following after Jesus. The Queen Mother had to bury her son, not in the limelight of millions of admiring, let alone adoring, followers, but practically alone in the silent eve, closing an ignominious death and rejection. Mary, Queen of Perfect Love, *help us…save us. Save souls!*

A Contemporary Role Model for this Virtue: Mary, Queen of Heaven and Earth; Still present daily in our lives.

We must be ever mindful that the Queen of Heaven can and will, by our petitions, maintain the inner peace of our souls, and her Son, Jesus Christ, will provide ample Grace for that. Candidly, there is not much many of us can do about a conflict thousands of miles away, but we can sure tend to the rising rage that threatens to consume us in our hearts and souls. This is true about all conflict, even those that arise from injustice.

Truly, we have a King and Queen of the universe, and all will be wonderful if we persevere. The world can only torment us for a very brief time. Still, there is more. We should be celebrating the City of God, and our citizenship there rather than hyperventilating about a truly short interval in the temporal world.

When we die, God will not ask how many voters we registered; which news stories to which we responded to with Scripture; what persons we helped elect; how we fought the enemies of the Republic.

The Queen of Heaven will not praise us for causes or extremist independence, but she will be so pleased if we bring to her a huge bouquet of flowers that represent all the persons we brought out of the coarse fields, especially those snuggled in patches of stink weed. Most of all, she will be so overjoyed that we managed to save ourselves.

In turn, how much gratitude will be owed to her for all her intercessions even when we were most prideful and rebellious.

No, we do not need to speak our mind , though we will do that, too.

We most definitely must speak our souls, and that refrain will bounce around the City of God forever, as will others who act similarly.

CONVERSION STORY

Mother to Mother (Overcoming women's abdication from their royal position in God's kingdom)

Katherine Burton was born into a German Lutheran family that rarely attended church. Following the path of agnostics, she married Harry, a failed Episcopalian minister, though the union would produce three children. Tragically, Harry committed suicide in the early 1950s.

While in her thirties, Katherine would meet Selden Delany, also an Episcopalian who himself converted to Catholicism and led her on a similar journey. Selden's book, Why Rome, reportedly provided the final spark for her to embrace of the Catholic Faith although some of her earlier poetry indicated that inclination already. Later, from 1933-1969, Katherine addressed issues of Catholic culture and Catholic feminine identity in a monthly column Woman to Woman in the Sign Magazine by the Passionate Fathers. Like Dorothy Day, later reviewers of her work would hone her views to be more modernist. However, among her causes was motherhood which she heralded as the greatest possible vocation even though times were most difficult for women to raise children. Still, she did recognize the possible rewards of outside work if feasible. A contemporary of hers, Dorthy Day, addressed the following which gives further insights. And note the similarities to our times nearly one-hundred years later:

Picketing

When the Campion Propaganda Committee went to picket before the office of the Mexican consul for the first time—and it was the first time Catholics in the country had ever picketed as Catholics—we asked those who were engaged in the work to recall Christ's way of the cross as they walked for Him. Once again Christ in His Mystical Body is being tortured and put to death, and we as Catholics were showing our silent grief and horror. When we go again in a body on December 12, the feast day of Our Lady of Guadalupe whose heart is once again being pierced with a sword—we can hold in mind also the death of the three men and the child (and more of the sixteen injured may be dead by now) who died for picketing the church in the state of Chiapas to prevent the army officers from going in and defiling the sacred place.

It is only by passive resistance that we can oppose our enemies. Picketing is a form of passive resistance to injustice.

In the United States there are the beginnings of what we are opposing in Mexico. We must protest now, while we have the opportunity. There is no use waiting until socialization of children is under way in the United States. The other day Mrs. Katherine Burton, who has a monthly page in The Sign, was visiting the office and she told us of educational trends in the public schools in Bronxville, New York. The courses in biology include detailed discussion of sex and birth control and this is for ten-year-old children—and the course is described as "from the amoeba to man." It sounds like Mexico!

Day, Dorothy. "Christmas" The Catholic Worker, December 1934, The Catholic Worker Movement. http://www.catholicworker.org/dorothyday/

Rosary Intentions

Pray the Queen of Heaven leads you, spouse (or close friend), family, neighbors (including perceived enemies or doubters), clergy and religious, educators, health care workers, business persons (including attorneys), politicians (elected, appointed, government employees), public figures (including communicators and entertainers) *to the Saints Court in the City of God.*

THE GLORIOUS MYSTERIES (Mark 16: 1-8; Acts: 1: 6-12; 2: 1-41; Rev. 12)

Fifth Decade *The Crowning of Mary as Queen: A great sign is given—we see the woman who is the mother of the child who will rule the whole earth with a rod of iron. She is crowned with strs and with the moon under her feet. (Rev. 12)* **For: Just Rule vs Earthly Monarchs.**

Add a personal faith quote or a prayer intention of your own at the end of this chapter to aid in your meditation:

_____
_____
_____
_____
_____
_____
_____
_____
_____
_____
_____
_____
_____
_____
_____

*Helping ourselves and others to **FAITHFULLY** follow Jesus Christ.*

Resources by Section and Chapter

NOTE: These sources present some examples of prayers, articles, books, encyclicals, internet sites, and associations or organizations. This first chapter emphasizes the Catholic Bible. Some particular sections of the Catholic Catechism will be noted in relation to each chapter theme.

The Catechism of the Catholic Church provides in each section and chapter of this book a treasure trove of insights and elaboration on Scripture, the Commandments, and Church teaching. (Of special note: Offenses Against Truth, CCC 2475-2487, addresses false witness, disrespect for a person's reputation, bragging, and lying. The Use of the Social Communications Media, CCC 2493-2499, covers the rightful role of media for the common good)

Of course, a Catholic Bible for Scriptural reading and studying is necessary. Choosing from A to Z almost literally may challenge readers as different, good Bibles, explore the Holy Word translated from different languages and commentaries. The Great Adventure Holy Bible through Ascension Press prepared by the Catholic Biblical Association, with ecclesiastical approval, is an easy to read Bible for young people as well. The Magnificat Magazine is another valuable resource full of knowledge but also spirituality.

Section One - Joyful Temperance - Chapter One

Prayer:

The Litany of Humility (catholictradition.org and other sites). Consider printing these prayers.

Article:

The Catholic Thing: The Canterbury Tales (Boswach) Francis X. Maier (Rage is self sustaining and always toxic) (Sirach 27:30)

Book:

Sarah, Robert Cardinal. *The Power of Silence: Against the Dictatorship of Noise.* (San Francisco: Ignatius Press, 2017)

Encyclical (www.vatican.va and www.papalencyclicals.net

Librates (Nature of Human Liberty), St. Pope Leo XIII, 1883

Internet Site:

http://www.carloacutis.com/en/association/mostra-miracoli-eucaristici

(Carlos Acutis National Apostolate)

Association or Organization:

Women Of Grace
Mailing Address:
PO BOX 15907
Clearwater, FL 33766 Phone:1-800-558-5452
Email: info@womenofgrace.com
Website: https://www.womenofgrace.com/

Section One - Joyful Temperance - Chapter Two

Various Sources:

Catechism of the Catholic Church: Of special note: 1825-1829; 1883-1885, *THE Second Command;* The Seventh Commandment; 2429; 243; 2446; but **many** more references

Prayer:

- The Divine Mercy Chaplet
- Prayer to St. Thomas More

Article:

- *The Catholic Thing* often addresses such topics and the commentaries are available on audio for the busy Catholic. Robert Royal's "Untimely Reflections on Hate (1/22/24) is one example.

- Online article: *Catholic Daily Reflections,* (https://catholic-daily-reflections.com/2021/06/20/the-judgmental-heart/

Book:

- Day, Dorothy. *Meditations* (Mahwah, NJ: Paulist Press, 1970).
- Thomas, OFS, Bret *Saint Francis of Assisi: Passion, Poverty, and the Man Who Transformed the Church* (Charlotte, NC: Tan Books, 2016).

Encyclical or Papal Letters:

Populorum Progressio (Development of People), Pope Paul VI, 1967

Internet Site:

juliagreeley.org (See conversion story)

Association or Organization:

St. Joseph Benedict Labre, the Holy Homeless One and Patron of the Mentally Ill. Visit the Guild: guildbjlabre.org for his story, the history of the Guild, and many prayer resources.

Section One - Joyful Temperance - Chapter Three

Various Sources:

Catechism of the Catholic Church, Of Special Note: Poverty of the Heart, CCC 2544-2550

Prayer:

- The prayer of St. Ignatius of Loyola for generosity (though in his spirituality, and attributed to him, the saint did not actually write it)
- "Prayer for the Holy Spirit's Guidance by Saint John Paul II" (See: *Prayers for the Moment,* Fr. Peter John Cameron, OP., Magnificat Press.

Article:

Online: *Witness to Modernity,* James F. Keating. January, 2024. (*https://www.firstthings.com/article/2024/01/witness-to-modernity*)

Book:

- Ames, CFR, Fr. Mark-Mary. *Habits for Holiness; Small Steps for Making Big Spiritual Progress* (Newark, NJ: Ascension Press, 2021).
- Drexelius, SJ, Fr. Jeremias. *Heliotropium: Conformity of the Human Will to the Divine* (Charlotte, NC: Tan Books, 1985)

Encyclical:

Le Pelerinage de Lourdes (Warning against materialism), Pope Pius XII, 1957

Internet Site

Human Life International, hli.org

Organization and Association

Society of St. Vincent de Paul

Section One - Joyful Temperance - Chapter Four
Various Sources:

Catechism of the Catholic Church, Of Special Note: Fourth Commandment, Moral Conscience, CCC 1776-1794.

Prayer:

Litany of the Holy Name of Jesus

Article:

Online: *Compulsory Feminism,* Scott Yenor, First Things, March 2024. (https://www.firstthings.com/article/2024/03/compulsory-feminism)

Book:

- *Sanctify Them in Truth: How the Church's Social Doctrine Addresses the Issues of Our Time* by Father Jeffrey Kirby, STD, Tan Books, particularly on the Section on Abortion and Preeminence and his devotional suggestion of reciting the Joyful Mysteries of the Rosary.
- *See Yourself As God Does; Understanding Holy Body Image Through Catholic Scripture,* Shannon Whitmore, Ascension Press.

Encyclical:

Exeunte Iam Anno (Right Ordering of Christian Life), Pope Leo XIII, 1888

Internet Site:

Return to Order, returntoorder.org

Organizations and Associations:

The Catholic Vote, catholicvote.org

Section One - Joyful Temperance - Chapter Five
Various Sources:

Catechism of the Catholic Church, Second Edition (of note: 1653, 2125, 2211, 2221, 2223, 2372)

Prayer:

Anima Christi

Article:

Magnificent Lecto Divina sources

Books

- Hershwitzky, Patricia. *Teaching the City of God in the City of Man: Pursuing Salvation Education* (St. Louis: En Route Books and Media, 2023).
- Salkeld, Brett. *Educating for Eternity: A Teacher's Companion for Making Every Class Catholic* (Huntington, IN: Our Sunday Visitor Books, 2022).
- Staudt, R. Jared. *Renewing Catholic Schools: How to Regain a Catholic Vision in a Secular Age* (Ventura, CA: Institute for Catholic Liberal Education, 2020).

Encyclical

- Divino Afflante Spiritu (Biblical Studying), Pope Pius XII, 1943
- Spectata Fides (Christian Education), Pope Leo XIII, 1885

Internet Site

ICLE, (https://catholicliberaleducation.org)

Organizations and Associations:

Avila Institute, avila-institute.org

Section Two - Luminous Prudence - Chapter One

Prayer:

Renewal of Baptismal Promises

Article:

- From Catholic World Report
- Online Article, National Catholic Register, August 2024: *9 More Church Fathers Explain the Catholic Belief About Baptism* See https://www.ncregister.com/blog/dave-armstrong-nine-church-fathers-on-baptism

Book:

- de Sales, St. Francis. *Introduction to the Devout Life.* https://www.catholicspiritualdirection.org/devoutlife.pdf
- Johnson, Fr. Josh, and Fr. Mike Schmitz. *Pocket Guide to the Sacrament of Reconciliation* (Newark, NJ: Ascension Press, 2021).
- Kelly, Matthew. *The Wisdom of Saints; 365 Days of Inspiration* (North Palm Beach, FL: Blue Sparrow Press, 2022).

Encyclical:

- *Acerbo Nimia (On Teaching Christin Doctrine), Pope Pius X April 15, 1905*

Internet Site

- Saint Titus Brandsma was a Dutch Catholic priest, Carmelite friar, professor, and journalist who opposed Nazi propaganda in Catholic newspapers. He was killed by lethal injection in Dachau in 1942. Website: https://www.titusbrandsmateksten.nl/

- Person and Identity Project (**personandidentity.com**)

Organization or Association

- The American Society for the Defense of Tradition, Family, and Property

Section Two - Luminous Prudence - Chapter Two
Various Sources:

The Catholic Catechism

Prayer:

Make Me An Instrument Of Your Peace, St. Francis of Assisi

Article:

Online Article: *Critical Grace Theory,* Carl. R. Trueman, First Things, November 2023. See (https://www.firstthings.com/article/2023/11/critical-grace-theory)

Book:

- Dumont, Pierre-Marie. *The Way of the Cross for Couples.* (Rome, Italy: Magnificat, 2019).
- Thigpen, Paul. *The Life of St. Joseph as Seen by the Mystics* (Charlotte, NC: Tan Books, 2022).

Encyclical:

Casti Connubi (Christ in Marriage), Pope Pius XI 1930

Internet Site:

Dan and Stephanie Burke (*spiritualdirection.com*)

Association or Organization

Society of the Little Flower (*littleflower.org*)

Section Two - Luminous Prudence - Chapter Three
Various Sources

Catholic Catechism of the Catholic Church

Prayer:

Give Us Hearts, Prayer composition by Fr. Dan Hartnett S.J. https://www.ssndcentralpacific.org/file/corporate-stance/immigration-reform-prayer-card.pdf

Article:

How Should Catholics Think About the Immigration Crisis? Kody W. Cooper, April 16, 2024. See online article: (https://www.wordonfire.org/articles/how-should-catholics-think-about-the-immigration-crisis/)

Book:

- Sheen, Fulton. *The Life of Christ* (Quick Time Press, 2020).

Encyclical:

Sapientiae Christianae (Christians as Citizens), Pope Leo XIII, 1890

Internet Site:

Catholic League (**catholicleague.org**)

Organization or Associations

Catholic Ministries Serving Migrants and Refugees (**USCCB.org**)

Section Two - Luminous Prudence - Chapter Four
Various Sources

Catholic Catechism

Prayer

- Hail, Holy Queen; Our Father
- —2 Peter 1:3-11

Article

The Ruth Institute Submission to the United Nations, Independent Expert on Sexual Orientation and Gender Identity (**ohchr.org**), March 9, 2021

"Riley Gaines Speaks "Biblical Truth About Men Competing Against Women, *Today's Catholic* , Archdiocese of Fort Wayne-South Bend, Indiana, Nicole Hahn, February 20, 2024

Book:

- Kelly, Matthew. *Beautiful Eucharist* (Annandale, VA: Wellspring Press, 2023)
- Von Hildebrand, Dietrich. *Transformation in Christ: Your path to salvation* (Manchester, NH: Sophia Institute Press, 1998).

Encyclical Papal Writing:

Man and Woman He Created Them: A Theology of the Body, St. Pope John Paul II

Internet Site:

Eden Invitation, Edeninvitation.com

Organizations and Associations

Father John Harvey Guild (frjohnharvey.com)
Sacramental Worldview for LGTB

Section Two - Luminous Prudence - Chapter Five

Prayer :

- Divine Mercy Chaplet
- Obsecro Te

Article:

- *The Weight of a Mass: A Tale of Faith (<u>catholicchildrensstories.com</u>)*

Book:

- Hahn, Scott. *The Lamb's Supper; The Mass As Heaven On Earth* (Garden City, NY: Doubleday, 1999).
- Pitre, Brant. *Jesus and The Jewish Roots of the Eucharist* with study guide (Greenwood Village, CO: Augustine Institute, 2011).

Encyclical

- *Mysterium Fidei (Holy Eucharist),* Pope Paul VI, 1965

Internet Site:

- Divine Mercy Daily divinemercydaily@marian.org

Organizations and Associations

- Eucharistic Congress

- Eucharisticrevival.com

Section Three - Sorrowful Fortitude - Chapter One
Various Sources:

The Gospels, the apostolic letters such as the Sermon on the Mount and the apostolic teachings.

Prayer:

- Act of Contrition—daily in the evening
- Prayer for the Intercession of St. Pio of Pietrelcina
- Seven Penitential Psalms, Magnificat August, 2023

Book:

- *Confessions,* St. Augustine. https://faculty.georgetown.edu/jod/augustine/conf.pdf
- Bertanzetti, Eileen Dunn, and Fr. Benedict J. Groeschel, C.F.R. *Praying In The Presence Of Our Lord With Padre Pio* (Huntington, IN: Our Sunday Visitor Publishing, 2004).

Encyclical:

- *Misericordia Dei (Sacrament of Penance)*, St. Pope John Paul II, 2002

Internet Site:

- Hallow (subscription and online phone app available)

Association or Organization

- Catholic Answers, <u>catholic.com</u>

Section Three - Sorrowful Fortitude - Chapter Two

Various Sources

- Catechism of the Catholic Church

Prayer:

- Nine Day Novena to the Unborn (USCCB)
- A Litany of Trust

Article:

- *What is Chasity and How Can I Be Chaste,* Thomas and Judy Licking with William Boudreau MD, CERC, August 2002

Book:

- Schmitz, Fr. Michael. *Made for Love: Same Sex Attractions and the Catholic Church* (San Francisco: Ignatius Press/Augustine Institute, 2017).

- Hershwitzky, Patricia. *The Third Millennium Woman* (Oak Lawn, IL: CMJ Marian Publisher, 2001).

Encyclical:

- *Christiannae Reipublicae (related to anti-Christian writing including pornography)*, Pope Clement XIII, 1766.

Internet Site:

Population Research Institute, pop. org

Organization or Association:

CourageRC (This may be in a different chapter...will relook)
Or
CERC (Catholic Education Resource Center) catholiceducation.org

Section Three - Sorrowful Fortitude - Chapter Three
Prayer:

The Act of Consecration for the United States
Surrender Prayer

Article:

Online article: *A Catholic Guide To The 4 Temperaments; Which One Are You?*, Good Catholic through The Catholic Company.

(https://www.goodcatholic.com/a-catholic-guide-to-the-four-temperaments/) This article also references a book called, *The Temperament God Gave You,* by Art Bennett, Laraine Bennett, Sophia Institute Press (2005)

Book:

- Ciszek, SJ, Walter J., and Daniel L Flaherty, SJ. *He Leadeth Me.* (Pittsburgh, PA: PRH Christian Publishing, 2014).
- Kerry, FSP, Margaret. *Live Christ! Give Christ!; Prayers For The New Evangelization* (St. Louis, MO: Pauline Press, 2015).

Encyclical

Christian Reconciliation, Pope Benedict XV

Internet Site

Pauline Books and Media, (https://paulinestore.com/)

Organization or Association

The Servites, the Secular Order
Order of the Servants of Mary under the title of Mother of Sorrows. secularservites.org

Section Three - Sorrowful Fortitude - Chapter Four
Prayer:

Stations of the Cross

Article:

Related to You Tube—Father Chad Rippenger
"The Passion"

Book:

- Thigpen, Paul. *Manual for Spiritual Warfare.* (Charlotte, NC: Tan Books, 2014).

Encyclical

- *Rerum Omnium Perturbationem (St. Francis de Sales),* Pope Pius XI, 1923.
- (Or On Doctrine of Modernists, Pope Pius X)

Internet Site

Catholic-Link, (https://catholic-link.org/)
mycatholic.life

Organization or Association

Holy Face Association, holyface.com

Section Three - Sorrowful Fortitude - Chapter Five

Prayer:

- The Magnificat (Canticle of Mary)
- The Seven Sorrows of Mary Chaplet

Article:

- Online Article: *Born Fundamentalist, Born Again Catholic,* David Currie, (September 26, 2011)
- The Coming Home Network International (https://chnetwork.org/answers-to-questions/salvation-2/)
- Shroud of Turin (the archeologist.org)

Book:

- Chervin, Ronda. *Taming The Lion Within* (St. Louis, MO: En Route Books and Media, 2017).
- *The Illustrated Gospels*, Magnificat Publishing, 2006.

Encyclical

Tamest Futura Prospicientibus (Jesus Christ Redeemer), Pope Leo XIII, 1900

Internet Site

The Coming Home Network International (https://chnetwork.org/)

Organization and Association

- Catholic365
- Covenant House

Section Four - Glorious Justice - Chapter One

Prayer:

Prayer on theological faith at Hymnary.org

Article:

Articles of Faith, *Catholic Answers,* Catholic.com

Book:

- Benedict XVI, Pope. *Fathers of the Church: Catecheses: St. Clement of Rome to St. Augustine of Hippo* (Grand Rapids, MI: Eerdmans Publishing Company, 2009).

Encyclical:

- *Pacem in Terris (Peace in Truth and Justice)* Pope John XXIII, 1963.

Internet Site:

In Ipso (God Within) in in-ipso.org. (to develop a more intimate relationship with Jesus Christ through prayer).

Organization or Association

- Knights of Columbus (Columbiettes) kofc.org; columbiettes.com

Section Four - Glorious Justice - Chapter Two

Prayer:

Prayer to St. Jude

Article

- *What Is Hope and Why Do You Need It* YouTube Father Mike Schmitz, Ascension.

Book:

- Hemler, Steven R. *Catholic Stories of Faith and Hope: How God Brings Good Out of Suffering* (Charlotte, NC: Tan Books, 2021).

Encyclical

Spe Salvi (In Hope We Are Saved), Pope Benedict XVI, 2007

Internet Site

Ascension Presents, Ascension Press.com

Organization or Association

- shrineofstjude.org

Section Four - Glorious Justice - Chapter Three

Prayer:

Come Holy Spirit, fill the hearts of thy faithful. Enkindle in them the fire of thy love. Send forth thy Spirit and they shall be created and renew the face of the Earth.

Article:

- Broom, OMV, Fr. Ed. (August 1, 2023). "The Holy Spirit's Seven Gifts to the Soul." *Catholic Exchange.* Online https://catholicexchange.com/the-holy-spirits-seven-gifts-to-the-soul/
- Article on evangelization in the modern world (i.e. Pope Paul VI, *Evangelli Nuntiandi*)

Book:

- Martinez, Luis M. *True Devotion to the Holy Spirit* (Manchester, NH: Sophia Institute Press, 2008).

Encyclical:

- *Divinum Illud Munus (Holy Spirit),* Pope Leo XIII, 1897

- Redemptoris Mater, Pope John Paul II, 1987

Internet Site:

- Word on Fire (Bishop Barron: wordonfire.org)

Organization or Association

- Abiding Together: A Podcast for Catholic Women abidingtogtherpodcast.com
- Exodus 90 for men. Exodus90.com

Section Four - Glorious Justice - Chapter Four
Prayer:

St. Gertrude Prayer for Souls in Purgatory

Article:

"Our Lady, the First Witness," *(the late) Fr. John Hardon S.J. Rosie Magazine,* Spring 2024

Book:

- O'Brien, Michael. *Island of the World* (San Francisco: Ignatius Press, 2010).

Encyclical:

Assumption, Pope Pius XII 1956 (See 1950)

Internet Site:

Bondi Ministries (reneebondi.com)

Organizations and Associations

The Association of Marian Helpers, thedivinemercy.org

Section Four - Glorious Justice - Chapter Five
Prayer:

The Magnificat

Article:

- Spencer, Susanna. *Mary, Queen of Heaven, Teaches Us to Long for Our Eternal Home.* Commentary, August 22, 2024, National Catholic Register ncregister.com

Book:

- Sri, Edward. *Queen Mother: A Biblical Theology of Mary's Queenship* (Steubenville, OH: Emmaus Road Publishing, 2005).

Encyclicals

Ad Caeli Reginam (Queenship of Mary), Pope Pius XII 1954

Internet Site:

The Blue Army, World Apostolate of Fatima, at the bluearmy.com

Organization or Association

Legion of Mary at legionofmary.ie

**Pray for us, O Holy Mother of God,
That we may be made worthy of the promises of Christ.**

All honor is given to God, the ultimate artist and painter. The glorious morning sunrise picture presented itself over El Dorado Hills, California. (2023) (This photo was taken by Mary Ott and is unfiltered.) For more information on *Speaking One's Soul* please visit our website at: https://www.cultivatingyoursoul.com

Pax Tecum

Patricia (Patti) Hershwitzky's Author Bio

Patricia (Patti) Hershwitzky, Ed.S., is the author of three other books: _The Third Millennium Woman_ (CMJ Catholic Books), _West Las Vegas_ (Arcadia Publications), and _Teaching the City of God in the City of Man_ (En Route Books and Media); articles in various Catholic periodicals and Catholic365; and numerous other published communications.

Mary Ott's Author Bio

Mary Ott is new to the Christian publishing environment. A cradle-Catholic and a graduate of a Catholic college in California, Mary fully returned to the Catholic faith in early 2023, after a personal experience which she calls "nothing short of a miracle." Following her illumination of conscience, she began a 'journey of the soul' back to Jesus.

While on this journey, she discovered her sister, Patti, was also a faith-soulmate, as well. Following hours of conversation with her sister about life as traditional women, wives, mothers, and grandmothers, along with discussing their differences and similarities, Mary and Patti began a mission to speak from their soul to others about how the modern world is a difficult pathway to walk as a faithful Catholic.

Fueled by a lifelong passion for writing, painting, photography, research, and genealogy after she retired from her business career in 2012, Mary combined her life experience and education skills to co-produce the book *Speaking One's Soul*. Their book also produced a website, www.cultivatingyoursoul.com, and a future podcast series called, "Cultivating Your Soul," which will align with the book's theme.

Currently involved in painting and doing her professional genealogy work, at her business, Before The Ink Fades, located in El Dorado Hills, California, Mary finds that her time is also currently devoted to writing another book. When she is not working, Mary spends valuable time with her husband, adult kids, and grandchildren.

Made in the USA
Columbia, SC
22 March 2025